Identity Crisis

Also by Stephen Frosh

The Politics of Psychoanalysis
Psychoanalysis and Psychology
Child Sexual Abuse (*with D. Glaser*)
The Politics of Mental Health (*with R. Banton, P. Clifford, J. Lousada and*
  J. Rosenthall)

Identity Crisis

Modernity, Psychoanalysis and the Self

STEPHEN FROSH

First published 1991 by
MACMILLAN PRESS LTD
Houndmills, Basingstoke, Hampshire RG21 6XS
and London
Companies and representatives
throughout the world

ISBN 0–333–51106–9 hardcover
ISBN 0–333–51107–7 paperback

A catalogue record for this book is available
from the British Library.

This book is printed on paper suitable for recycling and
made from fully managed and sustained forest sources.

10   9   8   7   6   5   4
06   05   04   03   02   01   00

Printed in Hong Kong

To my parents

Contents

Acknowledgements

Earlier and shorter versions of the chapters of this book have appeared in *Free Associations*, vol. 16, pp. 7–30 (1989), *Free Associations*, vol. 18, pp. 22–48 (1989) and in *Human Relations* (1990).

I would like to thank Daniel Miller for freely sharing some very productive ideas.

STEPHEN FROSH

Introduction

Psychoanalysis has never had more to say about contemporary culture than it has now. On the whole, however, it is not psychoanalysts who are saying it. The tradition of Freud's *Civilisation and its Discontents* has been taken up more by literary and cultural critics, by feminists and political theorists, than it has by psychoanalysts or psychologists. That tradition, of sweeping, poetic cultural criticism and analysis, thrives mainly on the fringes of psychoanalytic theory – amongst those who are not primarily clinicians, but who are concerned with making sense of the modern world and who feel the need for a compelling theory of subjectivity to help them on their way.

For something unexpected has happened in the social and political sciences, due in part at least to the advent of a body of sophisticated feminist theory. Politics has truly become personal; some might say, it has become so personal as to no longer be political. It is ideology which is now at the forefront of critical consciousness: how ideas, personal meanings and interpersonal relationships determine our experience and interpretation of the world, reproducing or subverting existing sets of power relations. Analysis of economic and structural features of society has given way to a hugely entertaining and occasionally illuminating 'discourse' on how the human subject – the experiencing 'I' of all our lives – is constructed in the midst of the flow and contradiction of social events. How, that is, we reflect in our own individual experience the dominating characteristics of the contemporary social environment.

Understanding and interpreting this experience requires a language and set of concepts which are finely attuned to the nuances of subjectivity. In particular, it demands a language able to grapple with psychological phenomena which are more extensive than those of consciously willed acts, a language that can reveal the unappreciated connections between what we experience and what it is we are. A language, therefore, of the

1

unconscious – of the impulses, anxieties, wishes and contradictory desires that are structured and restructured by our
immersion in the social order. Such a language is, of course,
the central component of psychoanalysis. In psychoanalysis, it
is the subjectivity of the individual which is the centre of
concern, a subjectivity given not just by what can be easily
expressed as a consciously available 'I', but also by obscure
and contradictory segments of a hidden self. For what is being
suggested is that the real persuasive power of the social
environment, its most enticing hold over our lives, resides
not in what it explicitly says to us, but in the way it enters
unbidden and unnoticed into the foundation stones of our
psychic structure. Social factors are *constructive*, in this view, in
a very simple yet subtle sense: they take the raw material of
each individual infant's basic psychological processes and weld
and order it into the shape of a particular structure of
consciousness and experience. This socially shaped structure
is sometimes called simply 'I', sometimes 'the ego', most
commonly 'the self'.

At its simplest, the self can be thought of as a psychological
structure that contains within it the various processes of mental
life; it is implicit in this idea that there is something organised,
stable and central about the self, that selfhood comprises a core
element of each individual's personality and subjective
existence. In addition, the self has an importantly ambiguous
status: it is both an object of knowledge and contemplation,
and an experiencing subject. I look out at the world from the
vantage point of my own self; I know what I am through
examination of the attributes of that self. What the relationship
between 'I' and 'self' is, it will be seen from this, is one of the
more complex conundrums thrown up by this ambiguity. 'I'
am my self, but I can know myself by reflection and
observation; on the other hand, under most conditions I
cannot know myself fully (because I am in my self); that is
why I need the psychoanalytic dialogue, in which I see myself
from the vantage point of the other. So an other can get closer
to my self than I can myself, even though I am embedded
within it and am the only one who has direct access to it. And
how does that other, the psychoanalyst, know anything about
the inner workings of my self? Because the analyst hears what I

say, sees what I do, and can make a judgement about the nature of the structure from which these things arise. Thus, the analyst can only reason my self into being; she or he can never observe it directly; I, on the other hand, am too close to it to see it all.

Different branches of psychoanalysis offer the whole gamut of modern attitudes here, from denial of the existence of the self to celebration of the 'true self' as the lasting refuge of honour and integrity in the face of modernity's sadism. One of the strands of this book is to investigate the consequences of these different attitudes towards the self; this issue is particularly germane to discussions of narcissism, often taken to be the most characteristic of contemporary psychopathologies. If you are narcissistic, it is claimed, you are struggling to preserve a shaky selfhood through the grandiose gratifications achieved by manipulating others; you also protect that self by avoiding dependency and real interpersonal relationships. Narcissism is not simple self-aggrandisement born out of an overvaluation of the self, but is more likely to be a desperate set of strategies for survival in a setting in which the self seems to be in danger of breaking down. This is, according to some theorists, even more strongly the case for so-called 'borderlines', whose selves have very little coherence; psychotic phenomena, it is further suggested, are the products of selves which have already collapsed.

This line of reasoning makes the achievement of selfhood crucial for mental health. However, others argue that the self, like the psychoanalytic 'ego', is an alienating fiction, produced as a defence against the painful realities of desire. The argument goes something like this: people are not really structured in stable, integrated ways but are, by nature, full of fluidity, contradiction, impulse and frustration, psychological processes brought together only to make coherence within the domains of rationality seem attainable. For that matter, rationality is itself an ideological fiction, imposed upon the irrationalities of psychological reality; intellect subordinating emotion, repression constraining desire. Under such circumstances, the formation of a self is solely a defensive manoeuvre; it may seem like mental health, but it is actually a way of limiting the subversive and poetic power of the unconscious.

Read like this, psychosis is not the ultimate breakdown, but the one true way to a breakthrough of desire.

Some of the arguments surrounding these differing points of view will be detailed in the main chapters of this book. What needs to be appreciated at the beginning, however, is that with very few exceptions psychoanalysts regard the self as a constructed phenomenon. This means that it is built up developmentally, through some mechanism or set of mechanisms linking interpersonal relationships with internal mental structures. The exact nature of these mechanisms differs from theory to theory, but a conventional account would place most weight on 'object relations' – on the way the child's early experiences with people or parts of people (the breast, in Melanie Klein's influential version) are absorbed as a set of fantasised internal relationships which become the building blocks of personality. This idea has two significant consequences for our appreciation of the conditions of selfhood. First, the existence of the self is made contingent; that is, it depends on the provision of certain circumstances that make it possible for an inner stability to be achieved. In most accounts, this achievement is regarded as, at best, precarious, requiring the continuing provision of what Winnicott famously calls 'good enough' relationships with others, in particular in early childhood. The absence of such conditions or their disruption by separations and other frustrating circumstances, or even more the presence of actively abusive elements in early relationships, means that the environment can turn persecutory rather than supportive. The consequences of this are that the internal structures are themselves full of persecutory elements, militating against the structuring of coherent selfhood. Depending on the severity of these conditions, various forms of self pathology can result.

The second consequence is related to this first one. The successful construction of a stable self depends on the fragile existence of certain supportive conditions; these conditions are interpersonal ones, themselves dependent to some degree on wider social circumstances. Therefore, any culturally pervasive pattern of selfhood can be seen as a kind of barometer of social processes, reflecting the quality of environmental conditions. Put more strongly, as the relative stability and integrity of the self is taken to be a product of the individual's history, in particular the quality of relationships in which she or he has been embedded, then if there are common characteristics of selfhood amongst members of any particular social group, it may be possible to use these as indicators of the overall quality of experience available in that group. If everyone is narcissistic, it suggests that the necessary conditions for the creation of a non-narcissistic self – conditions such as toleration of emotional intimacy and dependency demands – may have been socially eradicated. In this way, the characteristic state of self can be used as an index of the psychological adequacy of the cultural order. More generally, psychoanalysis is here being used not only to show how social conditions produce internal mental states and organisations of various kinds, but also to supply criteria by which modern social experience can be evaluated.

There are several dangers in this line of argument, of course. For instance, it is rather too easy to demarcate characterological disorders for the whole of society – 'cultures' of narcissism or psychosis, for example – by using the clinical categories of psychoanalysis loosely and liberally. This point is developed in some detail later in this book. In addition, the disagreements between different psychoanalytic schools on what are the necessary conditions for healthy development, and also on the form that that development takes, are so great as to make it difficult to move from descriptions of pathology to interpretations of their significance. One consequence of this is a brandishing of clinical terms as if they were weapons, with a consequent loss of critical clarity at all levels – political, cultural and psychological. Substantial care needs to be taken over the use of complex concepts if they are to become more than easy but meaningless polemical bullets. However, there is something important which many theorists seem to agree about and which may really touch on the characteristics of contemporary western life. This is that, whatever the self is, all selves are thrown into confusion when faced with the contradictions and multiplicities of modernity. Indeed, perhaps the most generally accepted characterisation of the modern state of mind is that it is a condition in which the 'struggle to be a self' is nearly impossible.

The modern mind

It is terms such as contradiction, fluidity, multiplicity which
come most readily to mind when conceptualising the contemporary experience of modernity. At least, this is the view of
most exponents of modernist and postmodernist movements:
that contemporary culture represents a rupture with the past,
throwing previous assumptions and traditions to the wind,
undermining accepted ideas and modes of relationship
between people and people, and between people and things.
Marx's phrase, 'all that is solid melts into air' is a kind of
emblem of this position, a position which partly represents
political and cultural analysis, but which is also partly an
expression of personal experience. For the conventional term
'alienation', describing the distance between a worker and the
product of her or his labour, does not completely catch the
essence of the modern state of mind. Alienation there certainly
is, and not just of the labour variety: it can also be used to
denote the difficulties confronting people's efforts to establish
links with others in societies in which traditional interpersonal
structures have disappeared, and the magnitude of the task of
mastering objects under conditions in which technology has
become extraordinarily complex and sophisticated. Objects
have lives of their own – self-programmable, unpredictable;
other people are equally mysterious and inscrutable; culture
itself changes in the blinking of an eye; what once was here and
now is gone, and our reluctance to acknowledge this is a sign of
our own dispensibility.

Here is the real terror and attraction of the modern
experience. The only stable state of being is instability –
openness to change, revolutionary transformation, catastrophic discontinuity. The real turmoil in the outside world is
mirrored internally, as it must be if there is any link between
the two orders. If the self is constructed through relations with
stable objects and dependable people, then it must be unsettled
when these objects keep disappearing, to be replaced by new,
exciting but equally disposable alternatives; and when these
people are themselves in turmoil, uncertain what thrills or
spills the world will bring next. Thrilling and spilling:
modernism proclaims the dangers of the abyss opened up by

the processes of modernisation, but also asserts the power that these processes make available to individual artistry and collective revolt. Postmodernism, on the other hand, denies that there is any depth of significance in these processes, but nevertheless celebrates the merry-go-round excitements of perpetual plurality. The differing claims and implications of these two movements will be sketched in Chapter 1; one thing they share, however, is the perception that the contemporary world is marked by dazzling speed of change and tumultuous technological, personal and political upheavals, and that these are experienced ambivalently – as exciting and threatening, and as all the things that 'destabilising' can mean.

Modern states of mind and forms of selfhood, then, are forged in the context of instability of a cataclysmic kind. This marks them with their own internal instabilities, opening the way both to pathologically defensive states and to a fluid and generative creativity. Openness to the modern experience can mean exhilaration in the multiplicity and heterogeneity of it all, but can also mean that the certainties of self slip away, leaving only a celebrating but empty surface. On the other hand, closing down and repudiating modernity may bring a sense of security, of knowing who one is, but at the price of having continuously to ward off the assaults of the new – of refusing to enjoy and learn from experience. And the extent to which a healthy compromise is possible, a compromise made up of openness to new influences and perceptions on the basis of a secure foundation of self, is a central problematic issue for both cultural and psychological theory. It may also, if these theories are right, be a central problem for every modern person.

Modernity, narcissism and psychosis

This is the outline context for the discussions that follow. Modernity is characterised by uncertainty, rapidity of change and kaleidoscopic juxtapositions of objects, people and events. Finding our uncertain way through these uncertainties is a prime task of contemporary existence, for individuals as well as for cultures as a whole. Some specific patterns of self-organisation may be linked with this modern state of affairs, particularly problematic structures in which the self is experienced as fragile and precarious. For this reason, there has been considerable interest amongst cultural theorists in psychoanalytically-described pathological self formations which seem to share the characteristics of an unstable or non-existent self structure – particularly the pathological formations called 'narcissism' and 'psychosis'. These are sometimes taken as products of contemporary social stressors, affecting only some individuals; but they are also often taken as emblems of the whole trajectory of contemporary culture.

The chapters which follow explore these intersections between cultural and psychological categories and try to discuss the extent to which each can helpfully be read in the light of the other. The particular dangers against which it is necessary to be protected come from two directions. First, there is a danger that accurate but broad and generalised perceptions, such as that of the difficulty of establishing roots for oneself at times of rapid change, may take the place of detailed psychological analyses. The consequence of this can be that clinical categories come to be used in an impressionistic rather than an exact sense, and we all become 'narcissists' or 'pychotics' willy-nilly. The complementary danger to this is that immersion in the analysis of some very specific clinical issues, for instance those facing patients with disorders of the self, can lead one to see parallels everywhere, until the whole culture becomes a symbol of pathology. What both these dangers involve is a slippage between categories that results in the richness of metaphor being mistaken for the dryness of identity; at its most virulent, there is a confusion between social and psychological levels of analysis. But this also points to the constructive possibilities to be found in this intersection of cultural and personal levels: that each can inform our understanding of the other and together produce an account of the *experience* of modernity – of what it is to be a modern 'subject', someone living in and struggling with the issues which contemporary culture produces.

These issues are, at times, relatively specific: they include race and gender as problematic divisions associated with profound oppressions; they also include poverty, enormous discrepancies in power and wealth, exploitation of some areas of the world by others. This raises a third danger: that these specific issues will be glossed over by analyses too concerned with grand theorising. As will be seen, there is very little coverage of intra- and cross-cultural divisions in the material to be discussed: on the whole, general accounts of culture, almost always meaning western 'first world' culture, are presented and mixed with descriptions of clinical states that neglect socially structuring elements such as class, gender and race. That it is possible for psychoanalysis to present intelligent accounts of these issues has been argued elsewhere (Frosh 1987, 1989); the effect of their neglect in the debates detailed here is one point which will be returned to in the Conclusion. But the strength of the generalising approach should also not be neglected: how it can produce insights which are potentially applicable to a wide range of people living under many cultural conditions, and also how it may have something to say about which of those conditions make it possible to really live, psychologically speaking, at all.

This book is divided into three major sections, each of two chapters. Chapters 1 and 2 outline the cultural debates within which current psychoanalytic theorising takes place. Chapter 1 focuses on the overlapping but somewhat opposed accounts of modernity given by modernists and postmodernists, while Chapter 2 investigates the parallels between these approaches and a range of psychoanalytic theories. Chapters 3 and 4 deal with narcissism: with the way it has been employed as a tool of cultural analysis, with the opposing valuations of narcissism, and with accounts of narcissistic pathology and the social conditions from which it arises. Chapters 5 and 6 move to a more extreme state, psychosis, and again discuss how this has been used as an emblem of contemporary culture, and how this usage fits in with a variety of psychoanalytic theories of what psychosis is all about. Overall, the book is an attempt to look critically at the way psychoanalytic ideas are used in cultural analysis whilst also examining the extent to which they have produced insights into the general psycho-cultural question of what the experience of modern living is like.

Chapter 1

Social Experience

At the end of Woody Allen's film *Manhattan*, the central character, Isaac, is lying on his couch sketching out an idea for a short story. He asks himself, 'why is life worth living?'. His answer is a muddle of minor cultural symbols: Groucho Marx, Willie Mays, the second movement of the Jupiter symphony, 'Potatohead Blues', Swedish movies, 'Sentimental Education', Marlon Brando, Frank Sinatra, Cézanne. But his thoughts stop with a more personal image: the face of his recently-rejected teenage girlfriend. He runs across town to find her again, catching her just as she is leaving to spend six months abroad. He asks her not to go, saying she'll get mixed up with too many new people and become somebody completely different, alien to him. She says, 'Not everybody gets corrupted. Look, you have to have a little faith in people.'

Towards the beginning of Marshall Berman's (1982) book on modernity, *All that is Solid Melts into Air*, there is a similar list, this time presented to demonstrate 'the brilliance and depth of living modernism – living in the work of Grass, Garcia Marquez, Fuentes, Cunningham, Nevelson, di Suvero, Kenzo Tange, Fassbinder, Herzog, Sembene, Robert Wilson, Philip Glass, Richard Foreman, Twyla Tharp, Maxine Hong Kingston' (p. 24). This list, like the entire book, is infused with a celebratory energy that marks deeply-felt personal enthusiasm. In the Preface to *All that is Solid Melts into Air*, however, Berman has already made known something more about himself. Shortly after the book was finished, he explains, his five-year-old son died. He writes of this tragedy in almost unbearably understated and intimate prose, linking it, with intense sensitivity, to the rhythms of modern experience. 'Those who are most happily at home in the modern world,' he says, 'may be most vulnerable to the demons that haunt it;

10

. . . the daily routine of playgrounds and bicycles, of shopping and eating and cleaning up, of ordinary hugs and kisses, may be not only infinitely joyous and beautiful but also infinitely precarious and fragile . . . .' But something is made even of this. Berman continues,

> Ivan Karamazov says that, more than anything else, the death of children makes him want to give back his ticket to the universe. But he does not give it back. He keeps on fighting and loving; he keeps on keeping on. (p. 14)

The trajectory of these two pieces is similar, despite the difference in the intensity of their emotional content. Both move from the external world of modernist cultural artefacts, experienced as life-enhancing and exhilarating, to the potentialities and realities of loss, and from there to an affirmation of relationships and the possibilities of human development. In both instances, this affirmation is far from Utopian. Indeed, it is minimal: having a little faith in people, keeping on keeping on. For both Allen and Berman, the external world – and specifically the modern urban environment – is a place of great beauty and excitement but also of threats and terrors. These threats are directed at the personal relationships from which we derive the supportive warmth that makes the harshness of reality tolerable: these precious relationships are precisely what can be taken away from us most easily and what we most dread losing. With them, when they go, go the underpinnings of our sense of self. A child whose father had left and whose mother had died, and whose therapy I was bringing to an end because I was changing jobs, said to me, 'Whenever somebody leaves, they take a bit of me with them'. What carries us through even this is a sense that we can only keep on keeping on – that our personal integrity allows us no other options than 'fighting and loving'.

These comments evoke a particular image of the surrounding physical and social environment and of the psychological responses which are appropriate to it. The image of the environment is of a setting in which human relationships are possible, but are always being undercut and destroyed. An environment in which personal integrity means something as a potentiality, but is always in danger of being fragmented by forces beyond our control. An environment, perhaps, to which fantasies of persecution are the legitimate response, but in which mental health is marked by the advent of depression, of a sense of the fullness of loving that is necessary for loss to be truly felt. Such 'healthy' depression can be seen all around. It is there in the maturity of an eight-year-old child whose mother has died, and who is capable of saying what each new encounter and parting means: 'Whenever somebody leaves, they take a bit of me with them'. It is there, too, in the stoical 'keep on keeping on' that expresses the affirmative vision of a creative father who has lost his son. Most generally of all, depression of this kind, built on the recognition of the reality of pain and loss and yet on the belief that it is worth creating and maintaining links with the world and relationships with others – depression of this kind is visible in all the efforts a person makes to construct a self which possesses some content, some energy, some particular individuality.

The important word here is *construct*. Who can tell what is 'real' in the human character, what pre-given, what invented? Much contemporary criticism documents the precarious standing of the 'self' which most of us take for granted – the self which we experience as the directing agent of our consciousness and the core of our being. Ordinary reflection makes each of us aware of the variations of self-presentation in which we engage and the extent to which we experience ourselves as not 'our self', as in some way artificial or self-alienated. Cognitive psychology emphasises how self-representations are built up from experience of our own and others' actions, showing how the self is not an automatically known thing, but an imagined entity the existence and nature of which is deduced from partial, often erroneous observations (Khilstrom and Cantor, 1984). Psychoanalysis goes furthest in decentralising and destabilising selfhood. What we know about ourselves, psychoanalysis suggests, is only a distorted fragment of the truth. Underlying it are the subversive operations of the unconscious, not in themselves integrated to form a particular 'selfhood' (although some psychoanalysts flirt with a 'true' but hidden self), but throbbing away with the energy of desire, in the extreme view reducing the status of the self to that of a cover-up or an expedience.

What is made apparent by these accounts is how the construction of a personal self, with a sense of autonomy and integrity, with moral and loving values, with an ability to form relationships with others – how this is a tremendous act of faith, an affirmation of the possibility of worthwhile existence in the face of the potential onslaughts of the destructive world. Richards' (1989) vision of the psychoanalytic project rings with precisely this faith: for him, it is 'to seek through the chaotic debris which necessarily constitutes a large part of modern experience, uncovering its abiding emotional content and trying, where necessary and possible, to reorder it around a core of meaningful selfhood' (p. 69). Creating a self is like creating a work of art: it may not be worked on as consciously, although sometimes it is (Miller, 1987), but just as art to some degree involves taking the bits and pieces of the world and fitting them together to say something, so does the self. The self, then, is an affirmation of what is humanly worthy and creative.

Or is it a pathological defence? That is, is it an illusion used to deny a reality which is experienced as too unbearable to face? This self, this creative affirmation in the teeth of the obvious destructiveness of contemporary society, is this a way of pretending that autonomy and integrity is possible, that the sources of distress are individual and that it is only moral fibre which needs to be improved for all to be well? And is this *pathological* because it prevents real progress by obscuring the way the conditions of the modern environment make selfhood impossible? This image of the self as an illusion suggests that the dissolution of the personality evident in some psychotic states should be seen as the purest expression of the human condition; or, at least, it makes psychosis a metaphor for contemporary experience. Just as the psychotic feels her or his self to be fragmented and in danger of death, and strives desperately to bolster it even at the price of creating a completely illusory identity, so each of us has some inner awareness of our own fragmentary, deconstructed state, and seeks refuge from this awareness in the illusion of wholeness. The closer to awareness we are, it seems, the more extreme and desperate are our attempts to cling on to the self. Psycho-analysis is right, in this account, to the extent that it reveals the machinations of desire and the speciousness of the productions of selfhood which the ego perpetrates. It becomes limited, ideological perhaps, when it goes further than this pure 'analytic attitude' and suggests alternative models of mental health in the acquisition of a new individuality – or of the kind of creative affirmations described above.

This book explores the resonances of the struggle for selfhood, using a psychoanalytic framework for understanding personal and social experience. These first two chapters offer an overview of the way different psychoanalytic approaches reflect different aspects of modernity; this overview is obviously sketchy, its aim being only to set the scene for the more detailed psychoanalytic account of the 'metaphors of the self' to be given later. And, as well as sketchy, the overview is crude. From a mass of sociological and cultural theory about the nature of modern life, theory which is articulated in a range of powerful presentations and a variety of voices (e.g. Baudrillard, Bourdieu, Hall, Lyotard), only one polarity is selected that makes some sense of the way the modern environment mixes its terrible violence with a kaleidoscopically thrilling range of experience, so continually presenting its face as both repellant and irresistible. This polarity, very loosely, runs between modernist and postmodernist theory. Its nature is more one of values than of description: that is, while modernism and postmodernism take radically distinct stances on the nature of reality and of human possibility, at the centre of both accounts there is a shared image of the fluidity of modernity, of the way it breaks down established notions of order in a threatening and exhilarating flow. It is this image which can be taken as a starting point for an exploration of the impact of 'modern times' on subjectivity – that is, the question of how the modern environment is experienced and what it comes to mean. Or, rephrasing the question marginally more precisely, 'What does it *feel* like to live in a world like this?'.

Modern times

Berman (1982) supplies an evocative portrayal of the modern experience.

To be modern is to find ourselves in an environment that promises us adventure, power, joy, growth, transformation of ourselves and the world – and, at the same time, that threatens to destroy everything we have, everything we know, everything we are . . . [Modernity] pours us all into a maelstrom of perpetual disintegration and renewal, of struggle and contradiction, of ambiguity and anguish. To be modern is to be part of a universe in which, as Marx said, 'all that is solid melts into air'. (p. 15)

Berman distinguishes between this *experience* of modernity and the processes of modernisation that have produced it, for instance industrialisation, urban growth, mass communications and – behind them all – 'an ever expanding, drastically fluctuating, world market' (p. 16). It is the disruption and destabilisation of the material and social environment resulting from modernisation that determines the peculiar agony of modernity – the irreducible mutual interpenetration of its terrors and excitements. The contemporary environment, in this vision, is both thrilling and threatening. Its more familiar, oppressive, face, lamented in radical politics and in humanistic therapy, is one in which people are crushed in the interests of industrialisation and profit. For some, this also represents a demolition at the hands of 'market forces' of the prospects for coherence and integrity of experience (e.g. Richards, 1989). But alongside this, operating at the same time and in the same space, are a set of new possibilities which modernisation makes available to people – possibilities of creativity and self-assertion that enrich the modern world as much as they express its ravages.

The process of modernisation, even as it exploits and torments us, brings our energies and imaginations to life, drives us to grasp and confront the world that modernisation makes, and to strive to make it our own. I believe that we and those who come after us will go on fighting to make ourselves at home in this world, even as the homes we have made, the modern street, the modern spirit, go on melting into air (Berman, 1982, p. 348).

This ability of individuals to assert their own creativity in the face of, and as part of the process of, modernisation, is *modernism*, the human and cultural response to modernisation and the experience of modernity. Modernism (documented with stunning virtuosity in Berman's *All that is Solid Melts into Air* by a range of work from Goethe to Maxine Hong Kingston, taking in Marx, Baudelaire and St Petersburg on the way) celebrates the excitement of perpetual change and also attempts to find a way of living with continually dissolving realities and fluctuating boundaries. It documents the destructive power of the social world and also the human possibilities which are inherent in it. It looks for the potential for self-development and personal affirmation which is available within the multiplicity of modern forms and forces. It is thus both a consolation and a process of empowerment. Modernism, in this view, whatever the tragedies with which it might deal, is an intensely optimistic set of ways of being and experiencing that feed back into modernity in heterogeneous modes of creativity and resistance.

It is important to maintain a grasp, however fragile it must be, of the explosiveness contained in the images of modernity arising from this vision. Modernism is about change: at its most literal, modernism is always the most recent theorisation and representation of experience, of necessity a critical engagement with what has come before – with the traditional or pre-modernist situation. Modernism is, therefore, always about the present, but it takes up its particular stance from an examination of the past. Moreover, it dramatises an awareness that the present is a temporary state, that modernity continues to update itself, that each new modern movement stands in a critical relationship to that which has gone before. Hence, as Eagleton (1986) points out, the 'typically modernist images of the vortex and the abyss, "vertical" irruptions into temporality within which forces swirl restlessly in an eclipse of linear time' (p. 139). Modernism is not about a stable state, but about the possibility for complete change – for both reconstruction and personal, cultural and political revolution. And modernism is *critical*: its awareness of the tragedies of modern existence arise from an image of people and of society as containing possibilities for development, possibilities which can be nurtured or squashed. Its criticism, therefore, can be scathing, as in the most powerful modernist images and texts; but it is never criticism for its own sake, it is always in the service of a vision of a possible alternative, of a state of being which is not so exploitative, degenerate, alienated or destructive. Modernism is, in this sense, a product of modernity, but one which, even as its products are appropriated into the 'high art' and commodity fetishism so characteristic of late capitalism (Eagleton, 1986), protests at the gap between what is and what might be.

Berman's (1982) stance on human possibility is embedded firmly in this optimistic vision òf how modernism operates. His history of modernism attempts to dramatise how modernisation

> nourished an amazing variety of visions and ideas that aim to make men and women the subjects as well as the objects of modernisation, to give them the power to change the world that is changing them, to make their way through the maelstrom and make it their own. (p. 16)

Being a human subject here means having a genuine capacity for production and elaboration of a personal self – a self which is a real expression of intentions and concerns. This self, historically speaking, develops in response to the economic and political contexts that surround it, through a process of internalising or appropriating the materials of culture and social relations in which the individual is embedded. Miller (1987), following Hegel, describes this procedure under the general heading of 'objectification' – 'a series of processes consisting of externalisation (self-alienation) and sublation (reabsorption) through which the subject of such a process is created and developed' (p. 12). Spelt out in more detail, this objectification model emphasises a dynamic of externalising and internalising, producing and consuming, through which the individual human subject acts on, and is acted on by, the material and social world.

As an intrinsic part of being, and in order to attempt an understanding of the world, the subject continually externalises outwards, producing forms or attaching itself to the structures through which form may be created . . . Although the subject may at certain periods appear lost in the sheer scale of its own products, or be subject to the cultural mediation of a dominant group, and thus fail to perceive these cultural forms as its own creations, the tendency is always towards some form of reappropriation through which the external can be sublated and therefore become part of the progressive development of the subject. (p. 180)

The experience of artistic, architectural and scientific modern-ism as *only* alienating and destructive, rather than as also constructive and creative, is theorised by Miller as a kind of misperception brought on by the scale and abstraction of the modern environment. This misperception is an instance of 'unhappy consciousness', a period 'in which we recognise the negative and abstract nature of these forces as oppressive, but fail to recognise that these negative conditions are an outcome of a whole series of historical developments which we otherwise regard as positive and essential for our well being' (p. 118). The full cycle of development, of both a culture and an individual, is one in which internal elements are projected outwards in material form, where they appear to sustain a life of their own – that is, where they appear to be alienated – but are then reabsorbed to enrich the inner being, increasing its complexity and also making sense of its experience. This image of development is one which, as Miller documents, can be found embedded in many theories drawn from a range of disciplines; in terms of individual development, however, it is particularly congruent with Kleinian psychoanalysis, with its emphasis on the projective and introjective processes that drive the child from the first period of life (see Frosh, 1987, chapter 5; 1989, chapter 2).

The account of subjectivity implicit in these modernist theories is one that suggests that individuals have within themselves an ability to respond to the tremendous momen-tum of modernisation by incorporation, by the construction of selves which contain aspects of, and feed back into, the production-consumption processes of modern capitalism.

Moreover, the existence of such selves, and of the modernist movements which they have produced, constitutes a spirit of resistance operating within modernity that holds out an alternative vision to the viciousness of much of contemporary reality. This spirit of resistance comes from the positing of a real self, a self which is not pre-given and fixed, as essentialist and biologistic theories might have it, but constructed and dialectical, with needs and desires which intertwine with the external world. But nevertheless a self which is *real*, not fictitious, and hence worthy of respect and of protection. That is, acceptance of the idea that the self exists presents limits to what can be justified in the name of material production and exploitation: it says, there is a human level beyond which people are not interchangeable, individuals have value, and their experiences – their subjectivity, however it comes about – have meaning and warrant respect.

Individuals, in this vision, are not fully constituted by the social processes that surround them. They share in the social, they experience modernity in all its fullness of promise and terror, but they are not identical with it. In each person there is something that can resist, something that can create, something that can appropriate the public sphere and make it home. Psychoanalytically, there is an ego which can become infused with loving values and with an ability to form constructive and reparative object relationships, in even the most dismal of circumstances. This ego can be swamped by the forces of modernity, but it can also be a bulwark against them. It can disappear into the chaos, or negotiate a rational and constructive path. The separation of individual and social and the way this combines with a belief in the power of the individual self to stand up to the ravages of modernity and to produce, in the face of despair, something of value – this is the theme that gives so many modernist texts their tragic power. Indeed, it is this theme that resolves the apparent contradiction between the remarkable optimism of theories of modernism, such as that of Berman, and the concentration on tragedy, destructiveness and loss which is characteristic of so much of the most significant modernist work – and of so many people's everyday experiences. For tragedy to be possible, for destructiveness to be meaningful and loss appreciated, there has to be something there that can be identified with, something that can love as well as lose, hope as well as be betrayed. In this something, this self, there is enduringly the spark of an optimistic resistance, a potential to respond in a humanly worthwhile way to the mess that is all around. Thus, in his reply to a critique by Anderson (1984), Berman (1984) reiterates the ambiguity of modernity, its mixture of passion and brutality. But it is what can be made of this that is his strongest, most affirmative theme:

> the people in the crowd are using and stretching their vital powers, their vision and brains and guts, to face the horrors; many of the things they do, just to get through day and night, reveal what Baudelaire called 'the heroism of modern life'. (p. 122)

Linking this version of the modernist vision with psycho-analysis, we are left with what Richards (1989) terms the Freudian 'philosophy of endurance'. Modernity, he suggests, is full of illusions, employed as protection against the devastating realities of contemporary urban experience.

> The most basic, persistent illusion is that other people do not exist, and that the individual can omnipotently avoid the pains of life which flow inevitably from our investments in and conflicts with other people, and from our biological vulnerability. To endure life is to endure the existence of others – which is also to endure oneself as a separate, conflicted individual. (p. 45)

As will be described later, this suggestion that modernity is characterised by the denial of relationships with others is a recurrent one in discussions of narcissism, both in individuals and as a cultural phenomenon. But the more general modernist proposition in Richards' quotation stands independently of the particular exigencies of narcissistic character structure: it is that the values of commitment to others and of toleration of reality, however painful it may be, are central elements in a truthful and therefore non-alienated existence. 'Endurance' therefore entails recognition and acceptance of the modern agony without recourse to escapist illusions. This is a characteristic image, for Freud as for other modernists; the question it raises, however, is: what if there is no reason for endurance, no real meaning underlying the modern kaleidoscope, to be recovered and preserved? What if the spectacular but empty surface is all that 'really' exists?

Postmodern states of mind

The image of modernity presented above evokes a world in which survival is constantly threatened by startling forces which have the power to turn everything upside down and to destroy those precious achievements of personal integrity and interpersonal affection towards which people strive. At the same time, it claims, the dizzying kaleidoscope of modern experience provides individuals with opportunities for development of their own capacities for representation and construction. These capacities are manifested through a process of reclaiming, or appropriation of, the public sphere for private uses; that is, individuals find means of expressing themselves through the same forces that threaten to engulf them. This process is loosely termed modernism and has produced not just some great works of art, but also lives lived as art – as constructive assertions of human possibility. In particular, the approach encompasses a vision of personal integrity through self-development which can survive the monstrous aggression of the world – which can 'keep on keeping on'. The self, constructed laboriously from elemental incorporations of cultural materials, is the centre of experience and the focus and source of resistance and creativity. This belief in the possible existence of a self is a central component of the mode of modernist reasoning described above; it is also precisely this image of the self and its potential for development which is called into question by the advent of what has come to be termed 'postmodernism'.

The complexity of the term 'postmodernism' and of the various forces which make up the postmodernist 'movement' is apparent from even a cursory overview of the various postmodernist sages. Hebdige (1988) notes, 'If the unity, the boundaries and the timing of modernism itself remain contentious issues, then postmodernism seems to defy any kind of critical consensus' (p. 183). Hebdige shows how the influential postmodernist theorist Lyotard has used the term in a variety of ways and how these contradict other uses by other writers – and, indeed, how the term is used differently in the USA than in Europe. Sometimes, the accounts of postmodernism are celebratory, conveying the excitement of the project of dismantling received certainties and also extolling the playfulness which is characteristic of some of the best postmodernist art. At other times, in other places, postmodernism has a critical edge, as an attempt to reveal the destructiveness of the contemporary obsession with surfaces and interchangeability, much as modernism opposes the destructive exploitativeness of the drive for progress. Moreover, postmodernism, by participating in the deconstruction of the self, can sometimes offer a fuller critique of oppression than does modernism. Postmodernism, in this post-structuralist guise, suggests that the illusion of selfhood bolsters the dominant order by allowing appeals to unchanging human nature and by locating the sources of potential resistance and, hence, responsibility within the individual. The postmodernist critique suggests, in contrast, that individuality is so permeated by sociality that there is no way of resisting on an individual level at all. More generally, postmodernism opposes all tendencies to take refuge in any illusion of wholeness or of received wisdom, even in aesthetic terms.

> The postmodern is that which, in the modern, puts forward the unpresentable in presentation itself; that which denies itself the solace of good forms, the consensus of a taste which would make it possible to share collectively the nostalgia for the unattainable; that which searches for new presentations, not in order to enjoy them but in order to impart a stronger sense of the unpresentable. (Lyotard, 1979, p. 81)

But this is rushing ahead, without identifying the important elements of the postmodernist account of contemporary experience. Lyotard (1989) describes three particular debates which can be distinguished in the term 'postmodern': first, the renunciation of 'a horizon of universalisation, of general emancipation before the eyes of postmodernist man' (p. 7); secondly, 'a sort of decay in the confidence placed by the two last centuries in the idea of progress' (p. 8); and thirdly, a process of self-reflectiveness, of 'working through . . . operated by modernity on itself' (p. 10). These overlap very closely with, and can be outlined with reference to, what Hebdige (1988) specifies as 'three closely linked negations which bind the compound of postmodernism together and thereby serve to distinguish it in an approximate sort of way from other adjacent "isms"' (p. 186). The first of these negations is an opposition to 'totalisation', defined as

> an antagonism to the 'generalising' aspirations of all those pre-Post-erous discourses which are associated with either the Enlightenment or the Western philosophical tradition – those discourses which set out to address a transcendental subject, to define an essential human nature, to prescribe a global human destiny or to proscribe collective human goals. (p. 186)

Lyotard summarises this position as: 'I define *postmodern* as incredulity towards metanarratives' (1979, p. xxiv). Large-scale theorising is replaced by detailed analysis of the separate moment in time and space, and of the specificity of the position from which that analysis arises. Thus, in Lyotard's (1979) examination of knowledge and legitimation in Western societies, he documents the decline of the narrative structures of traditional cultures. These narratives embody received knowledge, convey the social norms of their culture, and outline the mechanisms of application of social competence. They achieve legitimacy simply by the acts of speaking and hearing; that is, there is no need for an appeal to any particular legitimating process other than the fact that these narratives, these stories, have been told and heard in the past, by those who are telling them now. Contemporary western culture has to a considerable degree uprooted this form of customary knowledge, and science is intensely suspicious of it. Nevertheless, Lyotard suggests, science's claims to knowledge depend not just on the power of a particular investigative approach, but also on legitimation through employment of numerous 'little narratives' – the story of the discovery or the image of the scientist, for example. So, in post-industrial society and postmodernist culture, 'the grand narrative has lost its credibility regardless of what mode of unification it was, regardless of whether it is a speculative narrative or a narrative of emancipation'. However, 'the little narrative remains the quintessential form of imaginative invention, most particularly in science' (p. 60). As part of this anti-totalising suspicion of 'whole truths', subjectivity is recognised as entering into all discursive accounts of experience, but at the same time it is a subjectivity infused with the particularities of position, especially gender and race. Paradoxically, perhaps, postmodernism discounts the possibility of integrated theory ('postmodernism deflects attention away from the singular scrutinizing gaze of the semiologist and asks that this be replaced by a multiplicity of fragmented, and frequently interrupted, "looks"' – McRobbie, 1989, p. 165), but raises this argument for specificity and fragmentation to the status of a general critique of modernist and classical aspirations.

The second of Hebdige's 'three negations' is the one of greatest interest here. This he calls 'Against teleology', that is, 'a scepticism regarding the idea of decidable origins/causes' (p. 190), and most particularly of the notion that underlying the surface of events and experiences there are some 'deep causes', a set of origins which make sense of the surface and which can therefore be referred to as a source of explanations. This, of course, is the predominant mode of operation of traditional psychoanalysis: it is assumed that behind appearances there lies some deeper, unconscious desire which can be used to make sense of what that experience is. In Baudrillard's (1979) terms, the distinction is between 'seduction' and 'interpretation'. Interpretation, the activity of the psychoanalyst and of psychoanalytic theory, is a constant interrogation of appearances, asking what it is that lies behind them, what it is that gives them their form. It suggests that behind these appearances lies something more true, something which may become distorted but which, in principle at least, can always be recovered. Baudrillard writes, 'Interpretation is that which, shattering appearances and the play of manifest discourse, will

set meaning free by remaking connections with latent discourse' (1979, p. 149). As will be seen later, this is the crux of
the psychoanalytic vision. But Baudrillard suggests that
interpretation is by nature mistaken: 'getting beyond appearances is an impossible task', because every approach that
attempts to do this – including psychoanalysis – becomes
seduced by its own terms, forms and appearances, until it
becomes a kind of play on words, a set of investigations
devoted not to uncovering 'truth', but to persuading, deceiv-
ing, flattering others. And it is this 'seduction' which is,
according to Baudrillard, a central mechanism of the postmodernist process, a mechanism that works in the opposite
direction from the interpretive project.

> The havoc interpretation wreaks in the domain of appear-
> ances is incalculable, and its privileged quest for hidden
> meanings may be profoundly mistaken. For we needn't
> search in some beyond, in a *hinterwelt*, or in an uncon-
> scious, to find what diverts discourse. What actually dis-
> places it, 'seduces' it in the literal sense and makes it
> seductive, is its very appearance. (Baudrillard, 1979, p. 149)

This emphasis on the way all remnants of a 'depth' location
for the sources of experience has been lost in postmodernist
culture, is expressed with considerable force in Jameson's
(1984) seminal article, 'Postmodernism, or the Cultural Logic
of Late Capitalism', an article which is rather different from
either of the poles of unabashed celebration and ironic
disavowal that plague postmodernist work. Jameson's summary image of the postmodern experience can be found in the
conclusion to his description of what he calls a 'full-blown
postmodern building', the Bonaventura Hotel in Los Angeles.
This description centres on the dislocating sense of space
without fixed features that is the central element in the
Bonaventura's design. Jameson concludes,

> this latest mutation in space – postmodern hyperspace – has
> finally succeeded in transcending the capacities of the
> individual human body to locate itself, to organise its

immediate surroundings perceptually and cognitively to
map its position in a mappable external world. And I have
already suggested that this alarming disjunction point
between the body and its built environment . . . can itself
stand as the symbol and analogue of that even sharper
dilemma which is the incapacity of our minds, at least at
present, to map the great global multinational and
decentred communicational network in which we find
ourselves caught as individual subjects. (pp. 83–4)

It is the concentration on space that is at the centre of this
vision – the sense that the social world is made up of a confused
and crowded, but also immensely huge, network of movements
and random elements which are all of equal value, which have
no clear direction, and most of all no underlying essence or
history. Jameson illustrates this in a series of comparisons with
modernism, emphasising the surface-centredness of contemporary culture, its removal of affect and dismissal of previously
dominant 'depth' models of being, and most centrally the way
awareness of history gives way to a dazzling contemporaneity
in which everything is muddled together in a 'random
cannibalisation of all the styles of the past' (Jameson, 1984,
pp. 65–6). Where Berman, in his account of modernity,
proposes the possibility of real feeling when faced with the
threat which the modern world poses to personal relationships,
Jameson exposes the Warhol image of Marilyn Monroe,
commodified and endlessly repeated, devoid not only of
human warmth, but of any inner meaning. Whereas Berman
focuses on irony as the route to 'the deepest modern
seriousness' (p. 14), Jameson suggests that, in postmodernist
culture, 'pastiche eclipses parody' (p. 64); he explains this as
follows:

Pastiche is, like parody, the imitation of a peculiar mask,
speech in a dead language: but it is a neutral practice of
such mimicry, without any of the parody's ulterior motives
amputated of the satiric impulse, devoid of laughter and of
any conviction that alongside the abnormal tongue you have
momentarily borrowed, some healthy linguistic normality
still exists. (p. 65)

In Young's (1989) more caustic formulation, 'the post-modern seems to me to pronounce the jaded to be all we can have' (p. 87). Or Newman (1989, p. 141): 'postmodernist parody is closer to the cynical nihilism of fashion and the mass-culture industry: involving the implicit assertion that if everything is permitted then it makes no difference what we do and nothing is worth anything'.

There is no 'healthy normality' in postmodernism, no history that leads ineluctably forward. Instead, there is an eternally blinking surface, a space filled with television screens endlessly communicating indecipherable messages. A space in which there are no bearings, in which it is impossible to achieve any sense of distance – and certainly not the critical distance which is necessary both to modernist irony and to Freudian analytic progress. Indeed, like time, distance itself disappears in the postmodernist space. Jameson comments,

> We are submerged in its henceforth filled and suffused volumes to the point where our now postmodern bodies are bereft of spatial coordinates and practically (let alone theoretically) incapable of distantiation. (p. 87)

Looking inside oneself is no help: gone are the differentiations between the self and its expression, that make modernist self-development (and traditional psychoanalysis) possible. Instead of the individual author, planning and intending the product which becomes her or his art, there is a flow of practices variously called 'discourse' or 'text'. Meaning does not precede these practices, but is enigmatically created by them: the text is just itself, with nothing behind it – in Barthes' (1977, p. 149) famous formulation, 'a text's unity lies not in its origin but in its destination'. Instead of the self, producing its symptomatology as a compromise between underlying impulses and surface necessity, there is the random emission of desires, isolation of the present from the past and the future, schizophrenic intensification of each moment as it passes as something completely immediate, intensely exciting and devastatingly unreal.

The pessimism of the postmodernist position, implicit in this focus on seduction and appearance, 'simulation' in Baudrillard's version, comes also from its apparent relativity, a point which links with Hebdige's (1988) third 'negation', 'Against Utopia' – a 'strongly-marked vein of scepticism concerning any collective destination, global framework of prediction, any claims to envisage, for instance, the "ultimate mastery of nature", the "rational control of social forms", a "perfect state of being", "end of all (oppressive) powers"' (p. 196). Hebdige points, in this regard, to Lyotard's use of the notion of the 'sublime' as something which can never be fully known or rationalised. Baudrillard, too (e.g. 1976), can suggest no purpose or sense of direction which transcends the depthless-ness and interchangeability of contemporary culture; only death is different. Jameson (1984) actually opposes this political pessimism through a historical reading of culture and a belief in knowledge, which leaves open the hope of a fuller mapping of the social world in the future. 'The political form of postmodernism,' he writes, 'if there ever is any, will have as its vocation the invention and projection of a global cognitive mapping, on a social as well as a spatial scale' (p. 92). This mapping will be of what Lacanian psychoanalysts call the Symbolic, the order of language and culture that actually fixes the meaning of the experiences of the individual human subject. As such, its politics will be as much ideological practice as anything: identifying and understanding the discourses that frame reality in certain ways, presumably in order to begin to transcend them. Whether this is really an advance on traditional structuralist thought remains to be seen, however: if the subject is formed totally inside the system, fully penetrated and constructed by it, with no other source for its being, no inner opposition or values against which the quality of experience can be evaluated, then it is hard to see how there can ever be enough leverage for the system to shift.

Certainly, the leftist political critique of postmodernist theory has argued that postmodernism's celebration of the present as all that is possible merges into a valuing of what is given as all that one could want. Thus Eagleton (1986), on the anti-Marxism of this approach:

the postmodernism which celebrates kitsch and camp caricatures the Brechtian slogan by proclaiming not that the bad contains the good, but that the bad *is* good – or rather that both these 'metaphysical' terms have been decisively outmoded by a social order which is to be neither affirmed nor denounced but simply accepted. (p. 141)

Whereas modernism, with all its pained recognition of the difficulties of sustaining any form of 'authentic' being, presents some yardsticks for calibration of the worth or otherwise of any product or experience, postmodernism, particularly through its renunciation of history as anything more than 'a range of possible styles' (Eagleton, ibid.) offers no criteria by means of which any discriminations at all can be made. Everything that is is of the same value, meaning that there is no such thing as 'value', as a discriminating variable, at all. And by the same token, the demolition of any possible inner experience – anything of depth or interpretive significance – means that there is nothing that can be opposed to the contemporary state of the self, the fragmented, surface-obsessed, decentred, mirroring superficiality of being. As Eagleton points out, this is not another theory of alienation, because the concept of alienation suggests the possibility of some more authentic state from which one might be distanced. 'Those flattened surfaces and hollowed interiors are not "alienated" because there is no longer any subject to be alienated and nothing to be alienated from, "authenticity" having been less rejected than merely forgotten' (p. 132).

It is this forgetting of the past, this refusal to accept the possibility of any kind of 'value', this assumption that the deconstruction of received traditions of truth is the same as the demolition of all possibility of something other than appearances having meaning – these celebrations of seduction – that marks postmodernism as both anarchistic and also deeply troubling. For if this anti-truth theory is actually true, if nothing exists beyond the surface, beyond the immediate impulse for pleasure, the enjoyment of the moment of desire, then all attempts at understanding history are fraudulent – both the collective history of a people and its culture, and the private history of each individual self. Here Habermas' critique is relevant; Dews (1989) describes one of the central oppositions to the postmodernist and post-structuralist negations:

For Habermas, . . . it is not the *universality* of philosophical truth-claims which is to be abandoned, but rather their non-fallibilist aspects. Post-structuralism, however, is driven into an abandonment of systematic cognitive claims, indeed, because of its hostility to the universal, frequently into a quasi-aesthetic suspension of truth claims as such. The result of this manoeuvre, however, is that genuine attempts at social and cultural analysis become vulnerable to anecdotal and inadequately theorised evidence, a fact which explains the constitutive vagueness and portentousness of general accounts of postmodernity. (p. 37)

If everything is interchangeable then one is liberated from the requirements of acceptance of norms, traditions, earlier points of view; but there is also, unnervingly, nothing better to replace them with. On the other hand, what is often neglected in critiques of postmodernism is the explicit opposition of many serious postmodernists to the utilisation of art for reactionary ends, and their commitment to the preservation of certain human values. Whatever one thinks of his opposition to totalising theories, Lyotard himself makes some clear links between this stance and opposition to the fantasies underlying fascism. This is his conclusion to *The Postmodern Condition* (1979, pp. 81–2):

We have paid a high enough price for the nostalgia of the whole and the one, for the reconciliation of the concept and the sensible, of the transparent and the communicable experience. Under the general demand for slackening and for appeasement, we can hear the mutterings of the desire for a return of terror, for the realisation of the fantasy to share reality. The answer is: let us wage a war on totality; let us be witnesses to the unpresentable; let us activate the differences and save the honour of the name.

The various contrasts between modernist and postmodernist thought sketched in here centre on the attitude which they take up to the possibilities of resistance and self-construction within the context of a modern culture which is accepted as threatening and dangerous. For modernists, there is something in the depths of each individual, as well as real forces at work under the surface of society, which has the potential for destructiveness but which can also be used to resist the demoralisation and devastation with which it is always faced. This something appears in various aspects of material culture, notably in modernist creations, but is also visible in the experiences of self to which each of us clings as to a fragile lifeline. The self, as summary and integration of personal being, is not a fixed entity: it is constructed out of the bits and pieces of experience and is in a dialectical relationship with social organisation. It is full of conflict, particularly between what is desired and what is encountered. But in the distance there is a promise: not a certainty, but a chance that something more cohesive and supportive can be created.

The postmodernist vision is, on the whole, different. It is not totally negative, for it celebrates the excitement of modernity and the possibilities created by a culture swamped with material goods and permeated by communicational and computational networks which are usually impersonal, but which can be appropriated for play and innovation. But what it contradicts is any sense that there is some underlying intention or purpose to all these glittering surfaces, and, on the individual level, that there is something real and true lying behind the sense of self which is created within each individual. Postmodernism emphasises the fragmented nature of contemporary experience – fragments which are exciting but also meaningless in their interchangeability and lack of significant relationships. From this perspective, it is the *image* which is the most vibrant metaphor for modern reality: the image as on a television screen, with no substance behind it, creating, playing, disappearing, all in an instant gone. This image is subversive because it is fluid and provocative, but it is anarchistic because it offers no roots and no sources of value.

It is time to return to psychoanalysis, the real subject and object of this book. The next chapter is a brief survey of the connections which can be made between various important psychoanalytic traditions and the theories outlined so far. The main body of the book then takes two psychoanalytically-defined psychopathological states which have become metaphors for contemporary culture – narcissism and psychosis – and asks what they really have to do with the experience of modern living.

Chapter 2

Freud's Monster

For most people, psychoanalysis is still identified almost entirely with the figure, and work, of Sigmund Freud. It is Freud's image that stands out in bookstores; it is Freud who cultural historians, film-makers, novelists and cartoonists take as the embodiment of the psychoanalytic spirit; Freud is the psychoanalyst about whom far and away the largest quantity of biographical and popular essays are written. And it is the theories of Freud, if not Freud's writings themselves, which are explained, read, adulterated, construed and misinterpreted at a far greater rate, and in far more settings, than any other psychoanalytic work. Freud dominates the public face of psychoanalysis, and it is in relation to Freud's ideas, jumbled or accurately understood, that many people measure their own emotions and relationships.

But Freud is not fully of our time. His writings were contemporary with many of the originating works of the modernist movement and, indeed, informed much of the thinking of early twentieth-century artists. The great Freudian canon, still studied as the founding and basic texts of psychoanalytic theory and practice by psychoanalytic trainees, was completed over fifty years ago and is rooted in a set of dynamic models and assumptions reflective of a period fifty years before that. This does not, of course, mean that Freud's work cannot speak to contemporary audiences, for some of these models and assumptions remain potent, and all of them have had a formative influence over modern thought. Moreover, the construction of what Rieff (1959) calls 'psychological man', that self-centred entity of sensitivity and emotion, registering in the psyche all the affiliations and afflictions of culture, enacting internally the great pulsations and upheavals of the community – this is largely a creation of Freud's. But the times have changed and so too, in innumerable ways, has the set of institutions, ideas, theorists and practitioners that constitute the psychoanalytic movement. This movement was Freud's major legacy, even his progeny, second in importance only to his unalterable writings; but try though he did to fix its shape for all time, it has turned out to be a golem, with a life of its own.

Freud's monster has changed, developed, turned on its creator, chewed him over and spat out the unwanted bits, reverberated to more recent cultural changes, seduced itself with its internal politics, striven desperately to keep up with the times. These changes are significant, both for their potential truth value and for what they signify concerning the influences and forces which they reflect or which have produced them. The monster that is psychoanalysis has many heads, like all contemporary monsters; what makes each head alluring, seductive perhaps, is its claim to say something meaningful and revelatory about contemporary experience. More particularly, because psychoanalysis is rooted in the intense explorations of the consulting room, it takes up the central object of interest in the modern western world, the individual self of 'psychological man', and explores it in relation to its own subjectivity. So if the psychoanalytic monster speaks, it is as one who is privy to modernity's most personal secrets.

The dam metaphor

The changes which have occurred in psychoanalytic thought are partly a consequence of empirical and theoretical investigations into psychology and, to a lesser extent, culture, investigations which have forced revisions of developmental theory and elaborations of Freud's rather crude social psychological notions (see Frosh, 1989). But the main changes are probably due more to alterations in the clinical practices of psychoanalysts, brought about by demands for treatment from patients differing radically in symptomatology and psychic organisation from those described by Freud. The classic Freudian patients were hysterics and obsessional neurotics –

people with relatively clearly differentiated symptoms who might be understood to be suffering from too much repression. These people were not mad; they functioned on the ordinary human level which requires recognition of reality and the ability to form relationships with others. On the whole, they could manage this, but at an exaggerated cost. Like everyone else, their toleration of the demands of society required renunciation of certain inner demands, pressures for sexual and aggressive satisfaction which, if acted upon, would lead to the devastation of their social relationships and hence their selves. These inner demands, these 'drives', were theorised by Freud as basic, the fundamental inherited forces underlying all personality and motivation. Such a theory was, as many post-Freudian commentators have knowingly explained, rooted in some now-discredited assumptions of nineteenth century physics. But it was also rooted in Freud's experience of his patients' psychology, in the compulsiveness with which they sought out hurts, in the sense of being controlled by passions the nature of which they could barely perceive, let alone accept. The drive model may be out-dated scientifically, but it remains a common personal metaphor; what Freud felt, listening and struggling with his bourgeois neurotics, was their sense of the forceful flow of their inner desires as they began to burst the dams.

In this they were like everyone else; but the problem for these patients was that their underlying fixations and desires created unbearable anxieties, particularly centring on the destruction of self-control and of the ego-integrity which lies behind it. The cliché of the dam bursting was and is one by which millions lived and live their lives; the consequence of the resulting flood would be the overcoming of intellect by emotion, masculine order by feminine anarchy, rationality by irrationality, reason by desire. Primary and secondary process were the terms applied by Freud to roughly the poles of this opposition: primary process is the language of pleasure, the primitive assertion of wishes, chaotic and untrammelled; secondary process is the order the ego imposes on these, to make survival possible. Order and control: this is the language of the ego; according to Freud, it is also the essential bulwark against disintegration. Imposing order on the chaos of the unconscious is the task of civilisation and the individual project of all who live within it. So, too, is it the project of psychoanalysis: 'Where id was, there ego shall be: it is a work of culture – not unlike the draining of the Zuider Zee' (Freud, 1933, p. 112). It is this struggle, the struggle to maintain order in the face of threatening chaos, that characterises the life of the individual in society.

Freud's patients were no different from non-neurotics in adhering to the metaphor of the dam, but for them it was just that bit nearer bursting – their desires were that much nearer flooding through. As a last despairing attempt to preserve the ego against this force, they had dug some alternative channels; that is, the ego's defence mechanisms had reached a kind of compromise with the clamouring unconscious impulses, whereby the latter would be expressed, but in a sideways, displaced direction. This had the benefit of reducing the pressure whilst preserving the facade of the dam: it does not burst, but the water comes out nonetheless. So the pressure is eased, but the surrounding area is flooded: the problem with these substitute expressions of desire is that, being substitutes, they satisfy no-one. They neither accomplish the unconscious wish nor make reality tolerable, they are 'symptoms' of something unfulfilled, a pressure which, whilst made manageable, continues to exist.

> In this event the position, generally speaking, is that the instinctual impulse has found a substitute in spite of repression, but a substitute which is very much reduced, displaced and inhibited and which is no longer recognisable as a satisfaction. And when the substitutive satisfaction is carried out there is no sensation of pleasure; its carrying out has, instead, the quality of a compulsion. (Freud, 1926, p. 246)

Freud's neurotic patients were neurotic because their unconscious desires were so strong (mainly because of the particular form taken by their Oedipal experiences) and their defences so weak, that to survive at all they had to create a diversion into psychopathology; without it, their selves would disappear.

But with it they suffered, and so demanded help. Treatment was by means of the painstaking, repetitive 'detective task' of identifying and uncovering the disturbing repressed material that was placing so much pressure on the ego's defences. The mechanism of treatment was transference, the intense relationship of patient to therapist, in which the patient's unconscious impulses were played out and, eventually, openly expressed. The analyst's interpretations made sense of what was happening and promoted the process of 'working through', the linguistic recovery of hidden impulse, its conversion into secondary process form, and hence into something which could be controlled by the ego. The end point of therapy, therefore, was reached (if ever) when the patient's ego was freed from domination by unconscious forces, so that everyday life could be made smoother and richer. The dam is made secure, the waters are still there but more placid; desire is expressed to the optimum degree, repressed sufficiently to make survival possible.

These classical neurotic patients were the base upon which psychoanalytic theory was formulated; they have dominated cultural images of analysis from the start, as well as dictating the therapeutic techniques employed. In particular, switching away from the laborious metaphor of the dam, they embody the characteristic modern image of tension between surface and depth, between appearance and the real forces which lie beneath. For Freud, examination of the discourse of his patients revealed that there is a real turbulence of truth behind all ostensible acts, and that this truth – this set of underlying meanings – can make sense of what seems senseless and mad. Moreover, excavation of the truth, uncovering of the unconscious forces that 'really' govern behaviour, is a *therapeutic* task: it overturns the specious falsities of the everyday world, which is held together only through compromise and at a terrible cost to psychic health. So the undercover life of the unconscious is dangerous: its forces and formations pressing for expression constantly undermine the precarious relations between the self and the world. But it is also the source of truth, and it offers a possibility of change.

The notion that there is some interpretive depth reality which is more true than surface appearances is central to traditional psychoanalysis just as it is crucial to modernist views of creativity and resistance – and just as it is opposed to

the celebration of seduction that characterises much postmodernist criticism. It can also be detected in Freudian-based
analyses of the socio-political situation. Here, the surface-depth
model led first to Freud's 'Civilisation and its Discontents'
(1930), which emphasised the perpetual contradiction between
personal desires and social necessity, with the attendant
consequences of universal repression and the impossibility of
full human happiness. For Freud, the most that can be hoped
for is that individuals will learn to tolerate reality, and that
reality will be sufficiently tolerable to allow moderate
amelioration of pain. 'It is impossible,' Freud writes, 'to
overlook the extent to which civilisation is built upon a
renunciation of instinct, how much it presupposes precisely
the non-satisfaction . . . of powerful instincts' (1930, p. 286).
Underlying psychological stability are unmet desires; social
stability, too, is built on the renunciation of instinctual
impulses.

But this has been too negative for more politically committed
commentators. From the 'Sex-Pol' agit-prop of Wilhelm
Reich, to the careful Utopian readings of Freud developed
by Marcuse (1955) and Brown (1959), to more recent
recapitulations of psychoanalytic radicalism (e.g. Jacoby,
1975; Lerner, 1986), there has been a range of different
versions of the view that the liberation of humankind will
come with, or at least involve, the liberation of the repressed
drives. These latter theories are sometimes caricatured as a
'garden of delights' approach to human possibility, in the sense
that they present an image of human destiny as something
involving the free play of desire, untrammelled by the
exigencies of the social world. Full sexuality, in the Reichian
formulation, is a revolutionary state in itself, because it denies
the repressions of oppression – it rejects order and control in
favour of a barrier-less, exuberant celebration of desire. (As
will be seen later, some post-Lacanian feminist writers share
this imagery, even though their psychoanalytic base is
different.) Linked with social revolution, as it must be, a new
state of individuality could be envisaged which would allow
expression of what, under conditions of domination, remains
repressed. This, it is implied or claimed, would produce a truly
non-alienated state of self.

The limitations of these theories will not be dealt with in detail here (see Frosh, 1987, chapter 6 for a critical survey), for it is their provocative energy which is more interesting and worthy of note. The Utopian readings of the surface-depth, dam-busting metaphors of classical Freudianism derive their imaginative power from the general imagery and experience of *revolution*, the modern consciousness of the potential for radical overturning of the established order. The unconscious is envisaged as one of the creative forces that under the right circumstances can burst out from below, overcoming the restrictions, suppressions and repressions of what is taken for normality but is actually oppressive domination. Marcuse's approach in particular is a sophisticated and complexly dialectical one, but the aspect of the 'Freudian revolutionary' which is most compelling is the rather broad idea that the individual's struggle between underlying desire and surface necessity both expresses and reflects a wider social reality. As noted in Chapter 1, this is a crucial metaphor for the modernist movement: that behind the alienated surface lies something both brutal and exquisite. For both Freudian psychology and Utopian Freudian leftism, the underlying desire is more true than the surface necessity, because it consists of a set of human needs which are being kept unexpressed in the interests of domination masquerading as unchangeable reality. The way forward, therefore, is exposure of the defences, unravelling of the truth of desire, and a thorough bursting of the dam or – in another of these boundary-smashing images of change – volcanic upheaval.

In the cautious Freudian image, it is strengthening the ego, increasing rational self-control within a person, which is the mark of therapeutic improvement: a healthy world is one in which people behave towards one another with enough decorum to allow society to survive. Perhaps this really is a Victorian image; it certainly is linked to a recognition of the dangerous side of flamboyant change, the potential possessed by the modern world for destruction of all that raises humans above the level of brutes. For the Utopian leftists of the 1950s and 1960s, it was another aspect of this perception that was to be celebrated. People suffer from too much repression; liberation is the liberation of the drives, the full expression of all that we hold inside. Marcuse (1955), for instance, opposes the repressive structuring of the psyche with an exhortation to polymorphous perversity and the play of the sexual drives; this vision in isolation contains no detailed image of improved relationships, nor indeed of the kind of society that might make free expression of desires possible. Read unsympathetically, as, for instance, Fromm (1970) reads it, this concern with sexual liberation can be interpreted as an encouragement to individualism and perverse acting-out.

> Marcuse's revolutionary rhetoric obscures the irrational and anti-revolutionary character of his attitude. Like some avant-garde artists and writers from de Sade and Marinetti to the present, he is attracted by infantile regression, perversions and . . . in a more hidden way by destruction and hate. (Fromm, 1970, p. 31)

There is something true in this, but it is to be found in the subtext, the reference to a whole corpus of philosophical and artistic work which is troubling, subversive and exciting – which has the power to disturb. For what is missed in Fromm's assault is not just the specifics of the social theory which can be found elsewhere in Marcuse's work, but also a recognition that Marcuse and the artists with whom Fromm links him are responding to an accurate perception of something real in the modern world. They note the misery under which people live, but also celebrate the turbulence of modernity, the existence of driving forces and massive machines with the demonstrable ability to rip everything open, to completely transform the environment. The Freudian revolutionaries present a reading of the psyche in the light of this perception, as a source of equally massive forces, which need only to burst out for revolution to occur, for misery to be surpassed in a violent explosion of irresistible desire. What has to be recognised in this set of images is that even if it is a fantasy, it is a fantasy which has as its underpinnings the giant transformations of modern life; in this way, it is a genuinely modernist approach, a psychoanalytic response to the 'maelstrom'. Indeed, it can be argued that the entire 'depth' model on which traditional Freudian psychoanalysis is built – the image of underlying

desires and surface actions – reveals a modernist awareness of
the volcanic forces that threaten (and often manage) to turn
the whole world upside down.

Nature and unconscious passion

Through the power of these metaphors of nature – dams
bursting and volcanos erupting – the unconscious emerges as a
primeval entity, full of energy, held back only by the
controlling exigencies of culture. In many respects this is an
accurate reflection of the Freudian scheme: sexual and
aggressive drives are at best turned to the use of society
through the process of sublimation; at other times, they are
repressed or diverted from their aim, kept at bay in the
interests of the greater good. The ambivalence of this image
is at the forefront of radical Freudianism: as with all
revolutionary entities, the destructive and liberational elements go together. There is a danger, however, of romanticis-
ing the passion intrinsic to the Freudian unconscious, of seeing
it as 'natural' and therefore 'good', opposed to the adultera-
tions and constraints of normality. This was clearly not Freud's
view; if anything, he took the side of constraint in suggesting
that unconscious drives have to be tamed if society, and hence
the individuals which it protects, is to survive. There is, in
addition, a more subtle theme in the Freudian account of the
unconscious which again militates against a reading of it as
pure nature. As Freud's later id-ego-superego structural
scheme makes apparent, the 'unconscious' is not a place, but
a status given to certain ideas; these ideas are primarily the
psychological manifestations of the drives, and it is with them –
not the drives themselves – that psychoanalysis is mainly
concerned. Unconscious ideas are, according to Freud
(1915), 'thing-presentations'; they differ from conscious ideas

because they do not have 'word-presentations' attached to
them. Nevertheless, they are *ideas*, not actually things; that is,
they inhabit the world of thought, they are human, symbolic
entities. Kovel (1978) explains this clearly:

> The existence of the unconscious reflects the split between
> the human and natural world. The unconscious itself,

however, should not be thought of as a simple unmediated representative of 'nature' . . . The *thing* presentation refers to an event going on in the human mind, which, because it is a mind, is an entity that already has broken with nature. The *thing* presentation looks back at nature across the gap created when the self defined itself as distinct from its 'natural' primordium. (p. 103)

Unconscious ideas always operate in the space between nature and society, they are always a kind of formulation of what is lost as biological 'nature' takes up its place in a symbolised, psychosocial environment.

As one descends in to the unconscious world, recognisable social relations fade away and dissolve into primordial elements until they take upon themselves the thing-like form of unmediated nature . . . But the essence of Freud's position is not that mediation disappears completely, but that it occurs further back than the socially transcribed order can reach. (Kovel, 1986, p. 317)

One of the most substantial findings of psychoanalysis is that, as layer upon layer of unconscious ideas is uncovered through the analytic process, one never reaches a point of 'pure' nature, pure biology. At every level, whether it is the level of the inexpressible contemporary wish or the furthest-away infantile impulse, there is structuring of these unconscious elements – they take their place in the interpersonal, social world. The drives described by Freud might look 'objective', basic forces with no social roots, but what becomes of them – their subjective registration or meaning for the individual human subject – is always achieved socially. So, for example, there may be a biologically-derived sexual drive, but in its human form as sexuality it has a history that takes it through various organisational modes and interpersonal encounters – summarised as the oral, anal, phallic and genital stages. Sexuality is never experienced or manifested in a pure form; not only is it always mixed with aggression (Freud, 1920), but it is always explored and has meaning in the context of social relations.

The idea that the human subject is always separated from nature is taken up most forcefully in Lacanian psychoanalysis, to be outlined below (see also Frosh, 1987, chapter 5). What is most central here, however, is what happens to any notion of the 'passion' of the unconscious when it is seen not as a pure, subversive natural force, but as something which is already alienated from nature by being made human and psychological. Under the 'nature' formulation, unconscious elements of the psyche are revolutionary challenges to the social order, to be controlled or liberated according to one's political views. But if the essential symbolic mediation of unconscious functioning is recognised, a new question is raised: that of the qualities of the social field that give rise to different forms of personality organisation. This can be put at its strongest as follows. The existence of unconscious ideas undermines any notion of integrated personhood. However, unconscious ideas are not unstructured; they have their own mode of organisation, their own 'language'. The form this takes and the connections which are made between conscious and unconscious elements of the psyche, are achieved through a process of intersection between the individual and the social world. Biological drives may or may not originate 'within' the individual, but even if they do, they are transformed by the act of being taken up into the subject's mental space, in the context of the intense emotions of personal relatedness which exist from birth. This context, in turn, is organised by the structures of social life. Thus, both conscious and unconscious psychological functioning reflect the operations of the inter-personal context in which the individual is embedded; as this context is itself a part of the social setting, any meaningful opposition between nature and culture withers away. What remains is the infiltration of the former by the latter; the unconscious is not some oppositional principle, but a complex pattern of cultural relations.

Affirmative relations

It seems that the depth model is losing its hold over contemporary consciousness. Freudian 'psychological man' seeks to achieve a balance between inner impulse and outer control; the struggle for the individual is over how to function at ease with oneself, whilst also bowing to the requirements of social reality. This is a kind of 'citizenship' model of mental health, in which the priority is to carry out one's duties in order to share in the protection which society provides to its properly paid-up members. The individual's responsibility, towards the achievement of which psychoanalysis can help, is to manage her or his desires so that they do not obtrude noisily into the social realm. To keep oneself under control; or rather, given that it is *unconscious* passions that are the danger, to develop a self which is able to keep what is not-self, the id or 'it', quiet. Society, although it makes people unhappy by denying them their deepest wishes, is nevertheless in principle benevolent: according to Freud (1930), its function is to protect the individual against the dangers posed by nature and by what would otherwise be the uncontrolled impulses of other people. Society may, therefore, be oppressive if it does not provide its members with this minimal care, but it is not in an alienated relationship with the individual. That is, in the Freudian model, satisfactory self-control allows one to contract into a genuine social network, of which one is automatically part.

But self-control is no longer the issue. The problem now seems to be that whatever happens at the personal level, the gap between individual and social is virtually unbridgeable. Coping bravely with one's passions does not entitle one to anything, because it does not bear forcefully on the difficulty around which modernity really centres: the difficulty of moving out from oneself to make real links with others. Maintaining 'a little faith in people' is hard, but harder still is being trustworthy oneself. In part, this is because it remains difficult to avoid sexual or aggressive exploitation of others, as in the Freudian model. However, whereas Freud's description of the reasons for this difficulty was in terms of deep inner passions, the more contemporary perception seems to be not that people's desires are too deep and powerful to be fully controllable, but that people are too shallow to feel anything much at all – neither desire nor responsibility. The great 'getting in touch with oneself' fashions of the 1960s gave way to despair when, alongside other setbacks, it became clear that there was usually nothing inside with which to get in touch. Nothing, that is, except a terrifying sense of personal dissolution and an anger at the conditions that had produced this universal inner desert. So society is experienced not just as repressive, as Freudian citizens experience it, but also as outside, as a mirage; the relationship between self and other is non-existent, a gap reflecting both a lack of social ties and an internal, alienated absence.

This change, from the problems of too much depth to those of too much surface, has infiltrated psychoanalytic theory and practice too. In recent years, psychoanalysis in Britain and the United States has increasingly become dominated by object relations approaches and related variants. Ego psychology and 'classical', Freudian-based psychoanalysis remain important, and in Britain in particular Anna Freud's influence retains considerable power, but the primary focus of most work is on the object-relational quality – or lack of it – of the relationships formed by patients. Moreover, the language in which this work is couched is a language not of surface and depth, but of the quality of the self, a language that expresses the belief that it is problems of selfhood, of the *experience of being*, that underlie relationship difficulties. This language comes directly from object relations and Kleinian theorists, and it is interesting to note how notions such as 'true' and 'false' selves, internalisation, projection and splitting, are infiltrating even the work of psychoanalysts who continue to adhere to the classical Freudian tradition (Sandler, 1983; Greenberg and Mitchell, 1983). In the area of cultural applications of psychoanalysis, while there remain some hard-line reductionist Freudians who interpret aspects of, and responses to, modern life in terms of infantile drive fixations (e.g. Badcock, 1983), there has also been a growing reliance on interpersonal uses of concepts such as narcissism to ground explanations of contemporary conduct (e.g. Lasch, 1979, 1984; Richards, 1989) – a tendency which will be critically examined in the next section of this book. Particularly but not exclusively in radical circles, the influence of feminist object-relations theory has been profound (e.g. Chodorow, 1978; Eichenbaum and Orbach, 1982; Ernst and Maguire, 1987); its examination of the way unconscious but socially-formed images of femininity and masculinity are internalised and reproduced intergenerationally has created a new set of psycho-political perceptions and therapeutic practices.

These trends bear a direct relationship to the depth-to-surface movement described above. As people generally have experienced and expressed their worries less in terms of self control and more in terms of their inability to form satisfying relationships with others, so has this been reflected in the clinical practices of psychoanalysts. Over the post-Freudian period, there has been a gradual but marked broadening of the range of typical analysands, from people concerned with troubling unconscious desires, as in the classical images presented above, to people desperately seeking for a secure core of self – the central interest of object relations theory. Guntrip (1973, p. 148) supplies a characteristic description of such patients.

> They are the people who have very deep-seated doubts about the reality and viability of their very 'self', who are ultimately found to be suffering from various degrees of depersonalisation, unreality, the dread feeling of 'not belonging', of being fundamentally isolated and out of touch with the world . . . The problem here is not relations with other people but whether one has or is a self.

In the view of some object relational theorists (e.g. Fairbairn, 1944), problems of self underpin even the classical Oedipal difficulties described by Freud. This emphasises the claim that it is the establishment of a coherent self, not the control of desire, which is the central problematic area for modern individuals, with the excesses of impulse characteristic of Freudian patients being the result of their failures to form selves capable of healthy relations with others. For this is another element in the object relational argument: people's conscious experience is of the poverty of their relationships – commonly, their inability to love or trust others, or to give of themselves in any way, coupled with a feeling that the world is persecutory, that no-one else is to be trusted either. Thus, Freud's (1930) comment that 'not everyone is worthy of love' becomes 'no-one is worthy of love, nor capable of loving others'. But underlying this experience, its unconscious determinant, is a barely-glimpsed inner uncertainty of being. The inability to give of oneself derives from the fact that there is nothing to give.

This argument that problems of self underpin relationship difficulties, as in Guntrip's formulation of schizoid problems as 'not relations with other people but whether one has or is a self' is not, however, the whole story about the object relations position. The other side is the object relational assertion that the self is not completely pre-given, but is actually built up through relations with other people, particularly the mother. The somewhat different work of a variety of psychoanalysts adhering to this general point of view (e.g. Winnicott, 1956; Kohut, 1971; Kernberg, 1975) converge on the argument that it is damage caused to these relationships that leads on to the inadequacies of the self, which in turn produce narcissistic or schizoid symptomatology. This is one of the central ways in which object relations theory proposes a more open and interpersonal account of development than that offered by Freud: that is, it suggests that it is only possible to understand the individual in the light of her or his relationships with others, and that these are *constitutive* of the person's inner world. So the lack of self, which produces social relationship problems, derives in its turn from already-existing deficiencies in social relations themselves. This has some specific consequences for psychotherapy and for theories of personal and social change (Frosh, 1987), including the patterns of child rearing necessary for combatting sexism (e.g. Chodorow, 1978). However, the issue of concern here is the relationship between this kind of theory and the picture of modernity painted earlier.

The object relational perspective takes a major experience of alienation in the modern world and places it at the centre of its understanding of individual subjectivity. This alienation is of a particular kind. Without the ravages produced by society, object relations theorists tend to assume, individuals would be capable of intense and real relations with one another. Modernity, however, with its industrialised forms, its violence and its enforced separations between people, prevents the development of this relationship potential by imposing barriers between infant and adult, one person and another – barriers which are internalised and become organising principles around which the psyche is structured. So the presumed naturalness of contact between mother and child is broken by the rampaging demands of a society that values things more than people, that (in as poignant a definition of alienation as there can be) understands and treats people as things. This makes it impossible for any individual to experience the full satisfaction of their potential for relationships, and it is this dissatisfaction with personal being and achievement that leads individuals to experience their world in terms of dislocation and unbelonging – again alienated, modern experiences. To complete the intergenerational cycle, the stunting of human relations removes from people any sense of having a firm centre, a reliable source of values and balance; this lack of integrity and of integration makes it impossible for such an alienated being to support the development of another human self, richer and more healthily demanding.

The vision of modernity here is not the thrilling implosion-explosion model emphasised by Berman (1982), in which the terrorising elements are balanced both by the excitements of revolutionary change and the possibilities of individual resistance. From the object relational perspective, with its emphasis on the overriding importance of the two-person nurturing relationship, modernity is an assault on human need, perverting and distorting the rich possibilities inherent in every child. Furthermore, the remarkable manner in which the modern social world intrudes into every interpersonal encounter, however apparently private or trivial, makes the achievement of even a modicum of personal integrity and interpersonal satisfaction immensely problematic. At its most general, the social environment is theorised as threatening and alien, and all personal space for growth has to be rescued from it. Thus, for example, whereas classical Freudians regard the father as possessing major structuring importance in development, with the Oedipal situation being the crucible in which personality is formed, in Winnicott's theory the role of the father is mainly to protect the mother-child couple so that development can proceed without interference from social demands. Thus, what in one theory is seen as generative in the other is seen as a buffer: it is, object relations theory suggests, the two-person mothering relationship that holds all the seeds for healthy growth, if only it can be preserved intact. Human relationships, then, are central to self development, but they are not genuinely social relationships, for the social is always threatening to disrupt, to separate and to destroy.

In some ways, the object relational vision of a mythically whole mother-infant relationship is an impossibly romantic one, while the dangers of the external world are portrayed with the stereotyped quality of a projection. The political limitations of the hypervaluation of two-person over genuinely social relations, with its concomitant lack of awareness of the significance of social structure in influencing individual consciousness and experience, is also both clear and important for debates on the contribution of psychoanalysis to social theory (see Frosh, 1987). But object relations theory does also powerfully reflect a real and central aspect of modernity, mentioned at the beginning of this book: the sense that those relationships which are most precious and central to people are also those which are most vulnerable to the vicious forces at large in the world. They are vulnerable not only to corruption and disappointment, but to destruction and death. The description which object relations theorists propose of the schizoid state of mind is of a psyche in flight from the reality of this state of affairs, taking refuge in superficial and narcissistic relationships precisely because they are super-ficial, so that their inevitable loss will cause no pain. Depth remains dangerous, but in a different way from that presumed by Freud. It is not deep impulses that may be destructive, but the dependence produced by deep feelings, which must almost without fail lead to one being deeply, sometimes unbearably, hurt. So sticking to the surface, limiting one's investments in others (a typical contemporary metaphor) is safer, not just because it is excitingly, tantalisingly seductive, but also because it protects one against too much pain, even though the cost is that reliance on surface functioning leads to feeling dried up and dead. This is all presented by object relations theorists as a description of pathology and, generally speaking, in the context of a rather optimistic valuing of therapeutic possibility (that a 'real' relationship with a psychoanalyst can bring about significant changes in the schizoid patient, awakening the capacity for genuine links with others); but it is also a commentary on the way the modern world is increasingly experienced – as something outside us, over and above us, inexplicably alien and relentlessly threatening. Gone is the modernist celebration of the possibilities for self-development inherent in the terrors of change; instead, the only hope is to find rescue in a small island of understanding, parental-style interpersonal love, and to retreat from the damage the world brings. The regressive image of the mother-infant couple, protected from the demands and pains of reality, becomes the light at the end of the tunnel; it will be suggested in the next chapters that this is a truly narcissistic Utopia.

Bad world, mad world

It is worth comparing this set of images with those produced by Kleinian analysts. Kleinians also emphasise the relational context in which development occurs, and in that sense they can be categorised as object relations theorists. However, they are distinguished from psychoanalysts of the latter school by their view of the significance of libidinal and destructive drives, which are seen as the motors of development and thus as primary constituents of the psyche. Whilst the picture is complicated by the Kleinian assumption that the drives are always attached to specific objects, of which there is inherited knowledge, in general the argument is that inner states predominate over external ones, that the relationships which we form are always structured by internal, unconscious phantasies and desires, and that these mediate our experience of what the external world means.

It is the nature of the drives and of the mental processes accompanying them that distinguishes the Kleinian position from others. For Klein, at the centre of the infant's experience is the death drive, an inherited tendency towards dissolution and destruction, operating as the source of activity and disturbance, threatening the ego with total annihilation. It is the anxiety generated by this threat that motivates the infant's development, first into the world of object relationships and later into symbolisation and language. Thus, Klein (1946, p. 4) portrays the infant's initial experience of the world in cataclysmic terms:

> I hold that anxiety arises from the operation of the death instinct within the child, is felt as a fear of annihilation (death) and takes the form of fear of persecution. The fear of the destructive impulse seems to attach itself at once to an object – or rather it is experienced as the fear of an uncontrollable, overpowering object.

It is this anxiety that creates the need for the primordial defences of projection and introjection and the splitting to which they instantly give rise. According to Klein, people are born with death in their hearts; destructiveness and aggression are simply part of what it means to be human. This destructiveness is not immediately directed outwardly; rather, it is experienced as a terrifying inner force, made concrete in feelings of hatred and envy, directed at the infant's own ego, which it threatens to damage or even annihilate. The intolerable anxiety which this threat produces leads to the deployment of self-protective strategies in which destructive feelings are projected onto the external world (which thus becomes invested with persecutory powers) and only later, when they have been made safe by the supportive care of the mother, are taken back in and integrated with more positive, loving emotions. This is, in miniature, the full trajectory of development and indeed of mental health: from intense anxiety to projective and splitting defences that lead to the world being experienced as an abusive, threatening arena (the paranoid-schizoid position); to gradual integration of love and hate, with a tolerance of ambivalence, but with an acute awareness of the possibilities for loss and guilt (the depressive position). Finally, with the recognition of the internal sources of destructiveness and the damage which we can bring to those we love through the intensity of our passion, comes the creative force of reparation, defined by Klein as 'the variety of processes by which the ego feels it undoes harm done in phantasy, restores, preserves and revives objects' (1955, p. 133).

The relational stance of Kleinian psychoanalysis, coupled with its recognition of the reality of pain, destructiveness and loss and its emphasis on the processes by which integrity can be redeemed, have made it attractive to socialist commentators attempting to develop a non-individualistic position on human relations (e.g. Rustin, 1982). It can also, however, be read as a rather traditionalist assertion of the primacy of personal responsibility – that is, that it is the task of each individual to overcome the destructiveness which inhabits each of us, and to make something good of ourselves. In truth, the Kleinian position is a complex running together of both individualistic and socially-informed philosophies: the potential for destructiveness may lie within each individual, but the remedy is the creation of certain kinds of social relationships. Like object relations theorists, Kleinians emphasise the dangers inherent in existence; unlike them, they place the source of these dangers in the individual, as something deep-rooted, permanent and necessary. It is as a result of in-born destructive urges and the envy to which they give rise that development occurs; it is also these internal states that lead to the external world being experienced as threatening and terrorising. If anything, the Kleinian vision of the environment is of something which is safer than the infant's inner world: it possesses the ability to 'contain' the child's destructiveness sufficiently to make it tolerable and to reduce anxiety enough to allow for greater integration – a model both of mothering and of psychotherapy. It thus reverses the direction of object relations theory from a vision of the world as threatening and destructive of all that is most precious, to one in which it is a redeeming counterbalance to the destructiveness lurking within the human mind. Kleinians seem to be responding to the terrors of modernity by theorising them as necessary elements in human nature; it is then up to the individual, mediated and supported by the containment which a caring environment can provide, to make reparation for them – to produce creative and integrative acts and artefacts which symbolise the possibility of recovery from loss.

But here's the rub. The danger – and perhaps the common reality – is that the external environment will not be supportive enough to allow the progression from paranoid-schizoid to depressive positions to be achieved, leaving the individual terrorised by persecutory phantasies which may have internal origins, but which are confirmed by the brutality all around. Each loss then is a new inner devastation and reiteration of the power of the destructive impulse; that way not just narcissism, but madness lies. In the Kleinian vision, it is not that people flee from relationships to avoid getting hurt, but that they strive desperately for supportive relationships to stave off psychotic dissolution. Consequently, when one's paranoid anxieties are actually discovered to be the reality of the external world, the result is a desperate internal fragmentation and smashing into bits. The only way to survive, to preserve anything at all, is to chop the self up so fine, that nothing connects with anything else – a process described by Bion (1967) in his account of psychotic mechanisms and 'bizarre objects'. This preserves at least some bits of the self: as nothing connects, destruction of one thing does not necessarily result in the destruction of another. But the incredible augmentation of splitting that this flight from reality produces also has devastating subjective consequences. The world is experienced as weird and uncontrollable, full of concrete objects which are somehow imbued with personality and which are perceived as attacking and persecutory. And the self is a kind of rubble, every stone of which contains something important, but overall lacking integrity, its wholeness just a memory, its history despair.

Kleinian concepts often seem bizarre and unbelievable, but they possess the ability to convey an experience of the modern world as itself bizarre and unbelievable – an experience common to many people. It may indeed be that the degree to which Kleinians succeed in conjuring up the lack of containment to be found in the modern environment, and the subjective dislocation to which this gives rise, is a source of its growing intellectual and therapeutic popularity. Clearly, Kleinian theory engages with many images of modernity that are rife throughout our cultural consciousness, particularly in the ambivalent metaphor (and reality) of the 'machine': all-powerful, potentially able to serve, and yet totally and mysteriously disconnected from us and out of our control – another image of alienation, but an alienation which is full of the unbearable concreteness of psychosis. Our inner worlds are so fraught that they need a certain kind of environment to support them; modern society, with its buzzing confusions, its alienated surfaces and viciously penetrating violence, is on the whole not of this kind. Creative possibilities do exist: as in modernist theory, so in Kleinian thought there is an emphasis on the reparative potential within individuals – and for Kleinians it is reparation, rather than sublimation, that is at the root of the creative process. As long as destruction is balanced by love, envy by gratitude, so it is possible to feel depression and loss, to do more than flit superficially through an isolated existence. Rebuilding after destruction, making good, asserting the viability of the self: these are Kleinian virtues; depth remains. But when the terrors of modernity get out of control, as they so often do, there is no more prospect of integration, and everything, both self and other, becomes split, reified, unpredictable, empty and lost. Under this condition, both world and self are psychotically disconnected: there are small pellets of meaning, but they fire off in all directions, scattering the self uncollectably on the sands. No sense is left; the waste remains and kills.

Postmodern psychosis

In Chapter 1, the modernist perspective was presented as one that recognises both the destructive and affirmative elements in contemporary culture, stressing particularly the eruptive nature of modern social processes and the possibilities, fragile though they may at times be, for resistance and for personal creativity and integrity. This chapter has described how psychoanalysis reflects the impact of this vision of modernity in many of its own theories of contemporary subjectivity. Classical psychoanalysis focuses on the destructive power of uncontrolled unconscious forces and constructs a moral vision and a therapeutic order around assertions of the necessity for individual rationality and self control. Object relations

theorists perceive the centrality of personal relationships in
people's fantasies of survival in the modern world; they
emphasise the potential destructiveness of the external environment and the damage this can do to the possibilities of
nurture and of support for the infant's incipient selfhood.
Kleinians portray the terrors of existence with most verve:
having its origins within each one of us, destructiveness runs
riot if the environment is not built to contain and modify it.
The pathologies associated with these various positions are, for
Freudians, hysteria, compulsions and associated neurotic
states; for object relations theorists, narcissism and schizoid
personality phenomena; and for Kleinians, psychosis.

Despite the variations between these psychoanalytic positions, they share an attribute which is also common to the
modernist vision: a belief in the possibility of self-development
even in the face of the brutalities of modernisation. For
Freudians this self-development takes the form of personal
control and the utilisation of critical, rational faculties of
thought and knowledge. In object relations theory it is
centred on advocacy of a microsocial process of reclaiming
'real' and unalienated links with others that can allow the in-
born wholeness and sensitivity of the self to flourish. For
Kleinians, self-development involves toleration of ambivalence, recognition of one's capacity for destructiveness, and
the creation and implementation of a reparative faculty
dedicated to building and making good. Thus, even amongst
what sometimes appear to be pessimistic accounts of the
possibilities of personal stability, there is a theoretical affiliation to the potential for self-construction, for the creation of
some kind of personhood. Kovel (1978), who mixes an
appreciation of Freudian metapsychology with a creative
focus on the impact of the social field on individual development, expresses as follows this belief that construction is
possible even in the face of the deconstructions perpetrated
by the unconscious.

It is not the unconscious as much as the admission of a depth
dimension to subjectivity – 'psychic reality' – that tends to
dissolve the sense of personhood. That is to say, thinking
psychoanalytically, one comes upon self-experience in which

the categories of a coherent personality are no longer given, but from which they have to be achieved. (p. 93)

In a later essay, Kovel (1982) suggests that psychoanalysis' great challenge is its discovery of 'the radically repudiated underside of bourgeois existence', and that 'this discovery of Freud's enables us to regard any person, including ourselves, as an unfinished project, one whose real powers can transcend the given state of affairs' (p. 159). Even here, therefore, in what is a radical account of the subversiveness of the theory of the unconscious – its ability to undermine assumptions of personal integrity – and also of the constraints of social existence, there is a positive evaluation of the possibilities for transcendence, for the forging of something new, more whole and 'finished' than what is characteristically found.

All of the approaches described above are sustained by an implicit or explicit assumption of the potential for the construction of a meaningful self. All of them are, therefore, opposed by the postmodernist argument that the self is an impossibility, and that all seeming-selves are just that, glittering surfaces masking a litter of meaningless fragments. This opposition even applies to those elements in Kleinian theory, particularly in Bion's work (e.g. 1967), that focus on the sense of psychotic fragmentation which is one consequence of the ravages of modernity and which is given considerable significance by postmodernists. It is true that these Kleinian insights parallel in some respects the postmodernist vision of a world of surfaces, in which nothing has direction or significance; however, they differ from postmodernist theory in their suggestion that the motive for the ego's resort to extreme forms of splitting is to preserve at least something, some bits of the self, from the violence of the persecutory environment. That is, even though Kleinians recognise that a common modern state is to exist in fragments, they still believe in the possibility of the self, in the mental health goal of integration and meaning. Postmodernism disputes even this possibility and demands an approach to subjectivity that can cope with this position. It is in this strange context that Lacanian psychoanalysis has emerged as the most evocative account of the inner world of the postmodern human subject.

Jameson (1984), whose views on the depthlessness of postmodern culture were described in Chapter 1, notes the usefulness of the Lacanian concept of the signifying chain: the movement of signifiers that (rather than being the product of certain meanings or signifieds) produces the signified as an effect of its activity. Read simply, the signifying chain is the collection of signs that allows a meaningful representation of reality to be built. Experiencing this 'chain' as fully linked means experiencing the world as integrated and one's place in it as comprehensible and significant. When this signifying chain snaps, however, 'then we have schizophrenia in the form of a rubble of distinct and unrelated signifiers' (Jameson, 1984, p. 72). It is this snapping of the chain linking past, present and future that both modernists and postmodernists take to be characteristic of the modern experience. The difference lies in the analysis of the value and results of the ensuing fragmentation. For modernists, the snapping of the chain is a destructive act against which people rebel, lamenting the loss of self and the dissolution of the possible objects of their desires. The agony out of which creative modernism is born is precisely the filling in of the gap produced by this fragmentation – the subject of Berman's account. For postmodernists, the snapping of the chain is what reality is about – the contemporary sense of fragmentation is part of the disavowal of ideological illusions such as the autonomy of the personal self, a disavowal necessary if the true nature of the contemporary world is to be fully experienced.

Each group accosts the other and interprets their view as a psychic defence against reality. Young (1989), for instance, draws attention to the powerful psychoanalytic traditions mentioned earlier, principally object relations and Kleinian theory, with their assertion of the absolute necessity and value of the object and their analysis of the way the withdrawal of the self can be a defence against its destruction.

The work of these people [Kleinians and object relations psychoanalysts] allows us to take on board the phenomena of splitting, fragmentation and projecting the split-off bits – the unacceptable because despised or desired – and continue to perceive these and other psychotic mechanisms as part of, rather than an epitaph to, coherent, albeit damaged, object relations. (p. 88)

Postmodernist theory's celebration of the fragmented subject is seen here as a 'psychotic defence'; ironically (if irony is possible in postmodernism), this means that it has a meaningful function – to perpetuate the existence of the human subject and its relationships with objects, in the face of the despair produced by unacceptable reality. Put another way, postmodernism's critics suggest that its celebration of splitting and fragmentation is, in Bionian terms, a kind of smashing into bits, undertaken as a way of preserving something of value, albeit in a hidden and disconnected form. So, postmodernism undermines its own thesis: it claims that nothing has integrity or meaning, but the unconscious purpose of this claim is to raise a smokescreen that will allow something of integrity and meaning to survive. Thus far does psychoanalysing postmodernism take us.

Postmodernists, however, have their own psychoanalytic heavy artillery to appeal to. In particular, the Lacanian concept of the Imaginary, the order of experience which is concerned with the production of coherent images of reality, can be used to convey the manner in which people continue to strive to perceive the postmodernist world as if it made sense, as if it had origin and direction – when 'in fact' it does not. More strongly, the concept of the Imaginary focuses on the way the ungraspable nature of modernity produces such an intolerable sense of subjective fracturing, that the fiction of a central self which can control experience becomes necessary for personal survival. It is an 'as if' phenomenon: we relate to ourselves and to the world as if we and it are coherent and meaningful entities, because it is so difficult to do otherwise, but we lose sight of the fact that this is a metaphor for living, a pragmatic strategy, and start to believe – to hope – that it represents the truth, that we really are integrated and whole. So postmodernist theory, far from being a psychotic defence, is a robust refusal to have the wool pulled over our eyes, a firm statement that whatever illusions we may choose to employ to make ourselves feel better, they remain illusory, deceptive and false. Modernist theory is here the defence: if the reality of modernity is one of fragmentation and the dissolution of the subject, then belief in the integrity of the personal self is ideological, Imaginary, fantastic.

What both approaches grasp here, the one lamenting, the other celebratory or at least appreciative, is the tension between the energy of the constantly reiterating and reflecting images and surfaces of modernity, and the devastation of subjective collapse which these surfaces produce. It is this tension that makes the resonance of psychoanalytic theories of fragmentation so powerful. In the case of Lacanian theory, there is a further element that emphasises its congruence with the dislocations of contemporary experience. Lacanian theory's focus on representation, on how language structures the possibilities of personal and interpersonal experience, provides a metaphor for the radical babble of ideologies, messages and miscommunications which is a principal characteristic of modernity. This babble – the constant speech of mass media and computer, all different, all distorted – produces a set of competing discourses that are experienced subjectively as mysterious and confusing, but yet are constitutive of our consciousness of the world. It is perhaps this emphasis on incomprehension and 'misrecognition' that explains the peculiar appeal of the Lacanian approach, which in many respects remains incoherent (for instance in its account of language – see Archard, 1984) and indecipherable even to many of its admirers. The playfulness of Lacanian writing and speech, its slipperiness, its puns, its reliance on a stream of words the meaning of which cannot be pinned down, but somehow 'emerges' in an ungraspable way – all this is taken to reveal the reality of the modern state by acting it out and embodying it. Form generates substance: there is no fixed meaning, no one truth, 'no other to the Other', so theory itself becomes fragmented, partial and unstable. The form and structure of Lacanian thought is a kind of artistic mode, expressive of the postmodern condition as much in what it is as what it says.

There is, however, a substantive content to the Lacanian emphasis on representation that clarifies the postmodernist account. Lacan's theory focuses on the way the individual psyche is formed through a sequence of alienating splits that produce a semblance of internal integrity over an inner experience of fragmentation and emptiness. The two main points at which these splits occur are during the mirror phase (in which the ego is formed as an Imaginary fiction) and the accession to the Symbolic order (the set of relations that constitute culture), in which the individual becomes subjected to language. Both these points are organised around the penetration of the subject by something external – in the former case, by the fantasy of ego-wholeness encoded by the image in the mirror, in the latter by the smashing of this presumed integrity by the operations of the Oedipus complex, itself a carrier of language and culture. Put experientially, what this aspect of the theory communicates is the way the inner world of the individual is penetrated by overpowering external forces, felt to be uncontrollable, mystifying and alienating. Lacanian theory thus grasps an essential component of the postmodernist image: that we live in a world in which our selves cannot serve as a still and central point, because they have no fixed substance, and in which the social fabric cannot be construed because it is penetrated so fully by computational and communicational machines that produce only dread and well-founded paranoia. Subjectively, this process is experienced as a decentring of the self, an anguished recognition that there is nothing solid inside and that all our ways of construing reality are partial, contingent and marginal. 'All that is solid melts into air', as in Berman's formulation, but in postmodernism there is no way of combatting this, only of flowing with the tide.

This is in many ways a pessimistic view of the prospects for personal development, pessimistic in exactly the same way as postmodernist theory in general is pessimistic about social change. In the face of this pessimism, and the difficulties of accepting it – whether or not it is justified – it is perhaps not surprising that the post-Lacanian literature has produced opponents who use some of the concepts and linguistic tricks of Lacanianism, but contest its conclusions. The most important opposition of this kind has come from feminists, and has particularly taken the form of a rejection of Lacan's apparent assertion of the necessary domination of culture by the phallic, patriarchal order and the impossibility of any alternative mode of experience. Writers such as Hélène Cixous and Luce Irigaray have proposed instead an image of the fluidity and multiplicity of feminine sexuality which is presented as *another order*, as something radically distinct from, and freer than, the dead weight of the Lacanian father. Moreover, this femininity arises directly from the body; its rhythms and movements subvert the rigidities of the masculine order and install a new set of flowing experiences in its place. In the terms used here, there is a modernist element in this opposition to Lacan, pushing optimistically for a reclaiming of the alienated world and an announcement of the power of the previously disenfranchised woman to take experience and mould it in her own image. The emptiness of the subject as theorised in postmodernism, is counterposed by the vital fullness of positive desire. Cixous (1976), for example, opposes the concentration on lack in Lacanian thought with the following vision of feminine possibility:

> I don't want a penis to decorate my body with. But I do desire the other for the other, whole and entire, male or female; because living means wanting everything that is, everything that lives, and wanting it alive. Castration? Let others toy with. What's a desire originating from a lack? A pretty meagre desire. (p. 262)

The arrogance and contemptuousness of this passage is a reflection of its oppositional status, its hungry denunciation of Lacanian phallocentricity. But alongside this element is another one, a positive assertion of the possibility of full desire, of an impulse which has real content and can move towards satisfaction. A Lacanian reading of these assertions of fullness is that they are biologistic and reductionist (because of their emphasis on the female body as the source of desire), and that they set up an ideological romance of femininity (fluid, subversive, reproachable – the traditional terms used in male fetishising of womanhood) in place of a recognition of the reality of fragmentation and loss (e.g. Mitchell, 1982). Once again, this is a response that interprets theory as a defence against reality – in this case, self-ebullience as a cover-up for the dissolution of the self.

The central issue here is the same as the one that underpins the modernism-postmodernism dispute. All theorists recognise the intensity of the experience of fragmentation, dissolution and uprooting which characterises modernity. The differences arise in their response to this recognition. For modernists like Berman, alongside Kleinians and object relations theorists in psychoanalysis, the impact of modernity is to problematise selfhood, not to destroy it. The modernist project is to find a response, a way through the maelstrom, a tolerant realism imbued with non-utopian acceptance. The ironic stance of traditional modernism leads to a humane balance which aims only to 'have a little faith in people', to 'keep on keeping on', in the face of the ravages which modernity can bring. In ethical terms, this is a perception worth defending: a deeply moral and rational image of what can be retrieved through paying attention to our internal states and interpersonal relationships. Postmodernism reflects a further element of contemporary social experience, its slippery superficiality, which confuses and decentres, and leaves a taste of barrenness and profound alienation. The pessimism of postmodernist theory, however, derives not so much from this perception as from its totalising aspect: that is, the argument that this superficiality is *all that there is*, that resistance and self-assertion is no more than a mode of psychological defence. Modernists have their own response here, as documented earlier: they claim that those who dismantle the self do so in order to preserve the subject ('Many of the most Lacanian intellectuals are in Kleinian and Middle Group analyses. Each wants someone to love him or her best' – Young, 1989, p. 92). The post-Lacanian writers mentioned above go further, take the offensive against the negativity of the Lacanian order. They suggest that postmodernism, and with it Lacanian theory, is not only a defence against desire; it is also a mode of oppression that makes full desire – for instance, recognition of female sexuality – impossible. The extravagant and ebullient eccentricity of this work has its impact by smashing through the aridity of an approach that emphasises only alienation and distance. Post-Lacanianism often uses Lacanian terms, but it is not so abstract: it is about the material nature of personal rebellion, the potentiality of a violent, vibrant response.

To sum up briefly: psychoanalytic theories relate in many different ways to the experience which people have of the contemporary world. This experience is one of dislocation, alienation and fragmentation, of something which always threatens to run out. of control and destroy the precarious sense of self which we all try to maintain. The modernism of Kleinian and related psychoanalytic perspectives is moving and hopeful, and affecting on an individual level, because it is concerned with the resistance which each person can put up to the damage wrought by modernity. The postmodernism of Lacanian thought insistently questions our self-image because it is powerfully attuned to the sense of fragmentation and external control which is a real part of the structure of modern society. The post-Lacanian opposition holds excitement and promise because it shifts the emphasis from resistance to rebellion: it expresses the violence of modernity but with a liberational joy which has been missing from most recent debates. None of these strands of thought are completely wrong: a reason for their power is that they all reflect real aspects of modernity. But some are less defensive than others and some make more strategic sense. You pay your money and make your choice, in psychoanalysis as in other things. But with some choices you get the poetry of violence, with some you get a sense of despair and lack, and with some you may, if you are lucky, get some help in 'keeping on keeping on'.

Chapter 3

Narcissism

The culture of narcissism

Amongst the various writers who have employed the concept of narcissism to delineate a specific set of contemporary cultural and personal phenomena, it is perhaps Christopher Lasch who has been both most influential and most distinctively thought-provoking. Implicit in his work is an apparently conservative nostalgia for traditional modes of authority, particularly within the family (see Barrett and McIntosh, 1982, for a feminist critique of Lasch's work). However, the general thrust of his two major books on the subject, *The Culture of Narcissism* (1979) and *The Minimal Self* (1984) is to present a humanist case for self-regeneration, rooted in a selective reading of psychoanalytic theory. In doing so, Lasch constructs some important links between the nature of modern culture, in this instance American culture, and the formation of a certain type of subjectivity – in his view, an impoverished inner world.

In Lasch's reading of present-day experience, the major problem faced by people is that the conditions which are supplied by contemporary culture are not conducive to the formation of a deep and integrated sense of secure being, a self which is more than a collection of chameleon images. Lasch (1979) writes, 'every age develops its own peculiar forms of pathology, which express in exaggerated form its underlying character structure' (pp. 87–8). Our age's pathology is that of the character disorder and specifically of borderline and narcissistic states.

Studies of personality disorders that occupy the borderline between neurosis and psychosis, though written for clinicians and making no claims to shed light on social or cultural issues, depict a type of personality that ought to be immediately recognisable, in a more subdued form, to observers of the contemporary cultural scene: facile at managing the impressions he gives to others, ravenous for admiration but contemptuous of those he manipulates into providing it; unappeasably hungry for emotional experiences with which to fill an inner void; terrified of ageing and death. (p. 82)

Lasch suggests that this is the ideal type for bureaucratic organisations with narcissistic disorders being but exaggerations of the normal successful 'type' in western society. Everyday narcissists thrive in an environment that rewards manipulation of others whilst penalising the more personally expensive formation of intimate and genuinely caring relationships; such environments are perhaps characteristic of a certain type of pervasive social structure within modern political and financial arenas. However, the *cost* of such a mode of personality functioning is closer to Lasch's central concern – the way it results in, or derives from, distortions and lacunae in self formation which are experienced as deeply painful or even, at times, as cataclysmically and violently terrifying. It is this aspect of narcissism, its core component of inner impoverishment and desperate seeking after self, which has been the most compelling psychoanalytic extension to the common-language use of the term. That is, 'narcissism' is used in part to convey the egocentricity and rampant individualism of modern western ('consumer') culture; the psychoanalytic gloss which Lasch picks up on is to suggest that these are consequences and correlates of a deep sense of emptiness lying at the heart of contemporary culture and of the individuals who are part of it.

Lasch identifies a major facet of modern experience which has links with the pervasive cultural sense of ungraspable superficiality described in the previous chapters; this facet is close both to the myth of Narcissus and to clinically-described states of narcissistic and borderline discomfort.

> Modern life is so thoroughly mediated by electronic images
> that we cannot help responding to others as if their actions –
> and our own – were being recorded and simultaneously
> transmitted to an unseen audience or stored up for close
> scrutiny at some later time. (Lasch, 1979, p. 97)

The image of modernity is 'the image', expressed in the
language of television. Even more characteristically, Lasch
(1984, p. 33) defines narcissism in terms of a certain kind of
mirror function: 'a disposition to see the world as a mirror,
more particularly as a projection of one's own fears and
desires'. This point will be returned to in greater detail later,
but it is no accident that the imagery of the television screen
and the mirror dominates thinking about narcissistic states: it
is the surface representation of things, their appearance and
visual icon, which is valorised in a society concerned primarily
with the attractiveness of commodities – commodities whose
subtle differences have to be constantly emphasised to hide
their essential sameness. Lasch stresses the importance of visual
scrutiny as a kind of paranoid concomitant of existence that
permeates contemporary experience, a scrutiny ineradicably
linked with the necessities of capitalist production and, even
more centrally, consumption.

> The repeated experience of uneasy self-scrutiny, of submis-
> sion to expert judgement, of distrust of their own capacity to
> make intelligent decisions, either as producers or as
> consumers, colours people's perceptions both of themselves
> and of the world around them . . . Both as a worker and as
> a consumer, the individual learns not merely to measure
> himself against others but to see himself through others' eyes.
> (1984, p. 29)

This creates an intense concentration on surface and on
appearance, on the self as a set of images and roles, 'self-
presentation' as the core reality of experience. Symptomatic-
ally, some behaviourist theories take this at face value and
argue that the self is a post-hoc rationalisation, built out of
observations of one's own behaviour; for Lasch, in contrast, the

consequence of this surface-centredness is an alienated experience of unreality and inner emptiness.

> The mirror effect makes the subject an object; at the same
> time, it makes the world of objects an extension or projection
> of the self. It is misleading to characterise the culture of
> consumption as a culture dominated by things. The
> consumer lives surrounded not so much by things as by
> fantasies. He lives in a world that has no objective or
> independent existence and seems to exist only to gratify or
> thwart his desires. (1984, p. 30)

Richards (1989) takes this attack on the psychological value of
consumer culture a stage further, by suggesting that, through
its promotion of asocial omnipotent fantasies, it undermines
the stability and possibilities of formation of the self.

> There is little basis in successive acts of consumption for an
> individual's experience to cohere around stable configura-
> tions of feeling and value, and for the painful, affective
> interchange with other people upon which the development
> and sustenance of selfhood depends. (p. 65)

There are a number of themes here which recur throughout
this book: the relations between cultural and inner experience
is the main one, but also mirrors, consumption patterns,
distinctions between fantasy and reality, specification of the
actual needs of the individual. Lasch's work is just one
particularly influential example of an attempt to pull together
these various threads under the general rubric of an analysis of
contemporary social relations. Like writers in the modernist
tradition outlined in Chapter 1, his tone is critical and
dismayed, a kind of prophetic consciousness lamenting the
decline of the West; in Lasch's case, this is accentuated by a
more traditionalist regret at the dissolution of paternal
authority and the consequent withering away of moral
virtue, or at least of the super-ego. As will be described later,
this is a point of view that is shared by some important
psychoanalytic theorists of narcissism. But Lasch's work has a
number of other dimensions that lift it out of the sphere of

journalistic agonising over cultural decay. One of these is the breathless expansiveness of coverage: the two medium-sized books propel us through a dizzying kaleidoscope of modern issues, ranging from education to sport, politics to art, sex differences to consumerism, survivalism to the Holocaust. Or, rather, there is the sketching out of a small number of core ideas and then their application to this vast arena. In this respect, as a less high-brow version of Marshall Berman, Lasch embraces the energy of modernism: everything is engaged in with remarkable energy and zest; even in criticism there is some celebration. Moreover, everything is linked with everything else, all cultural commodities have the same story to tell. At its best, the form of this work expresses something about modernity that really is a powerful truth: its galloping speed, its enormous extent, the way it makes available an extraordinary array of experiences – and also, how everything comes out the same.

Another aspect of Lasch's analysis requires mention, however, and it is this that offers the provocation for the next two chapters. Lasch's evocation of the modern state of mind presents it as one in which superficiality and avoidance of intimacy are fundamental attitudes and in which the external world is experienced as an extension of the self – but an extension which has no more meaning than can be found in the depthless surface to which the self has been reduced. His powerful utilisation of the psychoanalytic notion of narcissism is the central element in this evocation and serves to link the particularities of modern western society – capitalist consumer society – with the internal, subjective states of meaninglessness and emptiness which he so charismatically describes. Narcissism, therefore, takes off from its clinical base; it becomes a diagnosis of collective experience and thence of social structure: western capitalism is 'the culture of narcissism'. The excitement of this lies in the way a notion (narcissism) which seems to resonate with common contemporary difficulties – the struggle to become a self and to form meaningful and trusting relationships with others – is used to make sense of the bewildering array of mysterious processes that characterise modern society. Thus, the conflicts with which each of us is familiar in our personal lives are shown to have some significance: they reflect the organisation of our world, we are part of a general cultural trend. Understanding this, perhaps we can change it; the creeping narcissism of our time may sometimes be fun, as self-aggrandisement sometimes is, but Lasch makes it clear why it must be opposed, for the end point of narcissism is not the triumph of the self, but its decay.

Many questions arise from this, particularly over what narcissism really is and the extent to which it can honestly be employed as an emblem for cultural experience. It is with these questions, and particularly with the substantive content of the varying psychoanalytic accounts of narcissism, that this chapter and the next are concerned. For a starting place, however, it is necessary to return to the issue of the self, paying special attention to its origins and to the way experience becomes internalised as the self is formed.

Subject and object

The notion of 'self' is an indeterminate one, used in many and varied uncertain ways. In ordinary speech, while most often the term is used just to position the speaker ('speaking for myself . . .'), it is also commonly employed to designate one's core experiencing agency or basic personal structure. To the extent that the term has currency within psychoanalysis, it is generally in a similar sense to this: as a descriptor of the whole personality, including areas both of conscious and unconscious functioning, with the particular connotation of a relatively permanent structure. This structure has a developmental history, one made up largely of transactions between inner impulses and external responses. The general thrust, however, is for theorists of the self to see its formation as something which unfolds in relation to environmental contingencies which may or may not be benevolent, this being the principal variable determining the final outcome of selfhood. What such benevolence and malevolence might be will be discussed below; but the process of self-construction needs to be filled in in slightly more detail to show just how fundamental is the place which must be given to what might be called 'procedures of incorporation' – processes of taking in the attributes of the external world and making them one's own.

Freud does not discuss the origins of the self, but he does write about the ego in ways which provide a rich entry into the question of how it is that experiences in the world become part of the structure of subjectivity. In the following passage, for example, Freud traces the impact of external frustrations and losses on the contents and character of the ego.

> When it happens that a person has to give up a sexual object, there quite often ensues an alteration of his ego which can only be described as a setting up of the object inside the ego, as it occurs in melancholia; the exact nature of this substitution is as yet unknown to us . . . At any rate the process, especially in the early phases of development, is a very frequent one, and makes it possible to suppose that the character of the ego is a precipitate of abandoned object-cathexes and that it contains the history of those object-cathexes. (Freud, 1923, p. 368)

When the desired aspects of the external world are beyond reach, as they always are in the end, they are absorbed into the psyche, they become part of the structure of the mind. The history of the ego is that it is 'a precipitate of abandoned object-cathexes' – a collection of bits and pieces, taken in in phantasy as they are lost in reality. The frustration of desire through loss of the object is deeply dangerous because it leaves the id burdened with a kind of angry energy – after all, in Freud's theory, the aim of a drive is to achieve satisfaction and it is through the object that this comes about. Under such circumstances, the fragile health of the personality is threatened with dissolution in the face of the unreleased energy of the drive, held back within the id; to save the whole, the ego prostitutes itself, offering itself in the place of the object.

> When the ego assumes the features of the object, it is forcing itself, so to speak, upon the id as a love-object and is trying to make good the id's loss by saying: 'Look, you can love me too – I am so like the object'. (ibid. p. 369)

Freud sees this 'transformation of object libido into narcissistic libido' as 'a kind of sublimation', perhaps 'the universal road to sublimation', and goes on to consider the implications of such a view for understanding the processes of identification and the super-ego in particular. But the phrase with most resonance here is, 'Look, you can love me too – I am so like the object'. Look, you can love me too: I am so desperate; my "I", my ego is so needy, I can be like the loved thing, I can be anything you want. Recognise me, but I am not a real me – I am like the object which has been lost'. This plea is a central one in the trajectories of narcissism: whatever is going on – whether self-aggrandisement, omnipotent phantasy, manipulativeness, shallowness – behind it is the despair of the attempt to be 'like the object', to attain the appearance of something worth loving, without ever being truly the thing itself. 'Narcissistic libido' is not just love for the self, but love that covers up a loss.

Freud always understood that the questions raised by narcissism are concerned with psychological structure. Recognition of the importance of narcissism was, for Freud, a source of his revisions to his structural model of the mind; it also played a crucial role in the reformulation of drive theory around an opposition between life and death rather than sexuality and ego-preservation (see Frosh, 1987). Indeed, the classic account in Freud's 1914 paper 'On Narcissism' reads completely differently in the light of the great later texts such as 'Beyond the Pleasure Principle' and 'The Ego and the Id', because their emphasis on the determining power of life and death drives and on the demands of the id and super-ego, raise the question of the reality and status of the ego. Especially when regarded in the context of its desperate attempts to appease these conflicting forces, what can the ego be if it has so little essence of its own, if it consists in such large part of discarded love objects, if it is so much a chameleon that, in its search for love, it can be anything at all? Later, in post-Freudian theory, the ego changes its form again, in notions of self and of object relationships; these are important changes, but the same questions remain. What strength has a self based on the internalisation of others, indeed, to what should we ascribe the sense of selfhood which each of us seems to have?

These are repetitive queries of contemporary experience: behind the mirror which the self needs to persuade it of its own existence, is there anything real? 'Look, you can love me too – I am so like the object'; possibly, I am so like everything that I am nothing at all.

Freud supplies a technical account of how what is outside might come inside: the ego takes on the characteristics of the lost love object. The increased emphasis on projection and introjection in the post-Freudian literature offers further insights. In particular, Klein emphasises the way the child's inner impulses are transformed through being mediated by a caring object ('container' in Bion's terms), thus portraying the early mother-infant nexus as a system which is characterised by the permeability of boundaries between what we take to be inner forces and external reality. Indeed, in Klein's account there is no clear distinction between the two: phantasy, defined as the unconscious mental representative of the drive, operates always, from the start of life – it is the way the mind works, so the generation of phantasies is a process in need of no explanation. Reality is only perceptible through the lens of this phantasy world, hence is always one step removed from objective status. What is inside can be experienced, through projection and projective identification, as if it is outside; hallucinations are an extreme form of this, but projection is also an ordinary fact of unconscious life. And what is outside, from wherever it originated (that is, whether or not it was originally a projection), can be taken back in, internalised and introjected. Identification is the least obscure instance of the mechanisms of internalisation: taking an attribute of the other as one's own or, more fully, developing a psychic structure which is an unconscious mirror of the object. Thus, one's own personality develops along the lines of construction perceived in the other; not just the world as mirror of the self, but the self as mirror of the world.

All this is healthy as well as unhealthy. According to Bion, what enables the infant's desperate aggression to be managed and integrated into her or his psyche, is the mother's ability to maintain a state of 'reverie' – an intense empathic connection with the child which nevertheless leaves the mother separate enough for her to retain her own emotional centre and hence to survive what might otherwise feel like murderous attacks. Klein's concept of the paranoid-schizoid position is *defined* by the way phantasies cross self-boundaries: the projection of destructive impulses into the object (the breast), their separation from more loving drives, and an experience of the external environment as constituted by persecutory objects alongside receptacles of hope. It is the ability of this 'environment' (the mother) to accept the aggressive projections without adopting a persecutory response in reality – more or less a characterisation of the state of reverie – that determines the degree to which the infant will feel held, will feel that her or his destructive phantasies can be tolerated and fully experienced without devastating the fragile infantile ego. A direct link with the other is imperative here: from mother to infant and infant to mother, something which traverses the material boundary between them – a boundary which is only provisional, in any case, given the feeding relationship.

This, too, is the understanding which Kleinians have of the mechanisms of therapy: that the pain of the patient is projected into the analyst, who holds, recognises and responds to it in such a way that it is 'contained' – that is, made less out of control, less dangerously rampant. The patient's ability to hear and appreciate this, to identify with the analyst's reverie and to receive back the projected parts of her or his self, completes a powerful cycle characterised by permeability of boundaries (or projection and introjection would not be possible) but also appreciation of difference and, to some extent, reality. This therapeutic possibility, built out of the ability of the mother to modify her infant's rage and of the analyst to contain that of the patient, is a critical manifestation of the psychological propensity to move outside of oneself in order to forge emotional links with others, but also to experience this 'outside' relationship as part of one's inner world.

Thus, Kleinian theory in particular, but other psychoanalytic approaches too (Freudian, object-relational, self-theories), have developed a sophisticated conceptual framework for appreciating the interpenetration of external experience with internal psychological structure. But perhaps, in essence, it is not so complicated. Everyone engages with the conditions of their own time and place; they are exposed to the world and their self forms in response to it. Everything that happens resonates on the subjective level; if it happens consistently enough, systematically enough, it becomes an element of structuration; that is, the inner world is formed along the axes which it provides. So it is with class, gender and race, the great structuring dominations of western society. So, too, with this conversion of 'object-libido into narcissistic libido'; or rather, the struggle to be a self. And in a mirror-fixated world, where appearance is what matters, it may be that there is a peculiarly difficult aspect to this struggle – it may be, for instance, that true 'reverie', which depends on the centring of the object's self in something deep and stable, becomes impossible. Without such a receptive object, such a still point of certainty and emotional reality, the infant cannot centre her or his own self. More specifically, psychoanalysis emphasises how the fortunes of ego and object are locked together; if one dies, so does the other. Hence the danger in the mirror: if everything is in the look, and if the object has value and specificity only in its surface, then so will the ego. 'I am so like the object' becomes, 'I am an image, nothing more'.

Narcissistic pathology

Kovel (1988) has written, about narcissistic personality states, that

> It is an odd feature of this disorder . . . that the diagnosis can only be made in a psychoanalytic setting. Any other context is simply unable to penetrate through the wall of pseudo-functioning thrown up by the narcissistic individual. (p. 194)

This goes quickly to the heart of the problem: narcissists seem normal – indeed, perhaps they are. In Kovel's own terms, it is a form of pseudo-functioning, what he calls 'de-sociation', which is characteristic not just of narcissistic pathology, but of all contemporary personality states. Narcissistically 'disturbed' individuals just show extreme versions of the contemporary alienated character, or, perhaps, they just happen to turn up at analysts' consulting rooms, asking for – and refusing – help. There, the intensity of the psychoanalytic encounter may be such as to reveal the desperation, fear and rage lurking behind the narcissist's character-armour. On the other hand, as will be suggested in the next chapter, the treatment received by narcissistic patients from psychoanalysts may well turn out to be a paradoxical variant on the social alienation which both parties are experiencing.

The more formal clinical descriptions of narcissism wobble on a difficult course between pathology and normality. Bromberg (1982, p. 439) inadvertently summarises some of the rewarded attributes of successful individuals when he notes, 'the defining qualities are most often described in the analytic literature as a triad of vanity, exhibitionism and arrogant ingratitude'. The first half of Kernberg's description (1966, p. 214) is similar:

> The main characteristics of these narcissistic personalities are grandiosity, extreme self-centredness and a remarkable absence of interest and empathy for others in spite of the fact that they are so eager to obtain admiration and approval from other people.

It is arguable, as indeed Lasch (1979) argues in the material quoted earlier in this chapter, that these characteristics of the narcissistic personality are precisely those required by a society in which it is the manipulation of others that paves the way for success. More strongly, in a world structured by its surfaces, a world in which it is the image of a thing which is experienced as its most real attribute, the exhibitionistic posturings of the narcissist and her or his freedom from emotional ties are attributes which come close to the ideal. Self-presentation, person-substitution, object replacement; a society of actors. In Bromberg's words, the location of the narcissist is 'between the mirror and the mask' – self-affirmation in the mirror, control of others from behind the mask (1982, p. 440).

Throughout the analytic descriptions of narcissistic patho-logy there is an emphasis on grandiosity and mirror-fixation, a mixture of an inflated image of the self and a need to have this image constantly confirmed by others. These are the attributes that dominate the relationships of the narcissistic person and are the source of the irritation which they provoke in others. Underlying them, however, is not a megalomaniac or even Machiavellian self-confidence, but a despairing sense of emptiness and fragility, of a self always in danger of dissolution and death. The following quotations from Morrison's (1986) collection convey this insubstantiality which lies behind the posturing and despair of the narcissistic character.

Unsublimated, erotized, manic self-inflation easily shifts to a feeling of utter dejection, of worthlessness, and to hypochondriacal anxieties. 'Narcissists' of this type thus suffer regularly from repetitive, violent oscillations of self-esteem. (Reich, 1960, p. 52)

Behind manifest grandiosity, depression is constantly lurking, and hiding behind a depressive mood there are often unconscious (or conscious but split off) fantasies of grandiosity. In fact, grandiosity is the defence against depression and depression is the defence against real pain over loss of the self. (Miller, 1979a, p. 328)

It is a quality of unrelatedness which represents the failure in development of a spontaneous, stable, taken-for-granted self experience. (Bromberg, 1982, p. 439)

Narcissism as a mode of psychological activity may represent a potentially healthy concern with the self and with self-esteem regulation and self representation; this point will be discussed later in the context of Kohut's theory and of Chasseguet-Smirgel's account of the relationships between the ego ideal and creativity. As a character disorder, however, narcissism is a description of the desperation of a self which has no content of its own. 'They are especially deficient,' says Kernberg (1970, p. 214), partially contradicting the quotation from Miller above, 'in genuine feelings of sadness and mournful longing; their incapacity for experiencing depressive reactions is a basic feature of their personalities'. As Kleinians have powerfully shown, the ability to feel depressive feelings – to experience loss, guilt and reparation – is a central designator of mental health, because it presupposes abilities to form committed relationships and to experience others as integrated, ambivalent objects. It is also dependent upon a reasonably successful negotiation of the paranoid-schizoid position, that is, upon an encounter with a maternal reverie that enables the infant's destructive impulses to be contained and that facilitates the projective-introjective processes described above. Saying that someone is incapable of experiencing depressive feelings is saying that she or he can only relate to others as imagos, as split-off, idealised or denigrated, reflections of a depreciated and unintegrated inner world. Moreover, at least in Kernberg's description, what lies behind the grandiosity and empty superficiality of the narcissistic personality is a rage characteristic, in Kleinian terms, of the earliest paranoid-schizoid levels of functioning. That is, it is not the case that narcissists have no object relationships, but that 'their interactions reflect very intense, primitive, internalised object relationships of a frightening kind and an incapacity to depend on internalised good objects' (Kernberg, 1966, p. 214). The superficiality of the narcissist, the lack of dependency on, and closeness to, others, is a defence against this agonising rage, a rage that, once mobilised, threatens to devour the fragile self.

So there is a mode of functioning, arguably characteristic of many individuals in the contemporary western world, designated by mirroring, by concern with surfaces, self-aggrandisement, manipulation of others, control. This mode of functioning reflects, feeds into, and is reciprocally produced by, those cultural conditions that emphasise the image, the superficiality of things (including relationships) and the interchangeability of objects of all kinds. Behind this mode of functioning, however, lies a different reality: of a dissolving self characterised by splitting, projected aggression and violence, and all-consuming rage. There are two possible, perhaps contradictory, links to be made here between personal and social experience. The first is close to the views of some object relations theorists (e.g. Winnicott, 1963): each human subject has an essence requiring expression in full and intimate relations with others; the failure of the modern world to supply the conditions making such relationships possible, results in a thwarting of the natural potential of the self and a resulting rage. A more politicised variant of this reading makes certain positive human capacities natural, their distortion a product of social conditions of domination and alienation. The second reading of the person-social link makes less of an appeal to an atomised human nature by claiming that each society constructs human subjects in its own image. What narcissistic rage reveals is that, behind the superficial aggrandisement and glamour of modern culture lies a violence always threatening to erupt, always projected and materialised in modes of oppression and domination. Racism is an example, as Kovel describes (1984, p. xcvii):

> The racist relation is one . . . in which the white self is created out of the violation of the black self, through its inclusion and degradation. Racism degrades the Other to constitute the dominant self, and its social order.

The white self does not exist without reference to the black, but the kind of existence it has is one built on degradation and repression of the other. More generally, in a world in which there is no security or depth of self, the continued existence of the self can only be supported through constant buttressing involving denigration of the other – that is, by way of a phantasised expulsion of one's own destructive despair into the object. Becoming 'powerful' in this unreal way depends on destroying the unsettling difference represented by the other – projecting one's own weakness into the other and then denying the link. This is a possible model for a general defence against the terrifying fluidity of the modern world.

Narcissism begins to appear here as just one example of the violence that contemporary culture perpetrates upon human potential, a violence with which each of us has to struggle in order to survive. The particular nature of the violence expressed in narcissistic pathology is modernity's disruption of the conditions in which the growth of a secure self might be rooted – conditions which in this discussion, following Klein and Bion, have been called reverie and containment. But there is some more work to be done here on the possible mechanisms through which narcissism takes its hold – mechanisms which have to do with mental structure as well as process.

Lost illusions

Many formulations of narcissism perceive it as the manifestation of a deep longing for a lost state of oneness – that 'oceanic feeling', a critique of which forms the beginning of Freud's (1930) 'Civilisation and its Discontents'. There, the oceanic feeling, held by some to be the origin of religion, is traced to the early development of the ego. The suggestion is that in early infancy, no boundary is experienced between ego and object.

> Or, to put it more correctly, originally the ego includes everything, later it separates off the external world from itself. Our present ego-feeling is, therefore, only a shrunken residue of a much more inclusive – indeed an all-embracing – feeling which corresponded to a more intimate bond between the ego and the world about it. (p. 255)

We remember our oneness with the universe – with the experiential universe of early childhood, that is, with the mother. This memory remains in an inarticulate, unconscious form, an 'ego-feeling' which nevertheless gives rise to powerfully emotive states and is associated with deeply held religious convictions and experiences. It is, therefore, a living memory; acted out in full, as Freud notes, in states of being 'in love', but often partially present in waking phantasies of wholeness and unification – phantasies of reparation and rejuvenation, perhaps.

Freud treats all this with some respect, but his acknowledgement of the normality of this state of affairs is vitiated when he writes, 'I cannot discover this "oceanic" feeling in myself' (p. 252). As an atheist, he has rooted out all the superstitious traces of mystical religiosity; as a rationalist and self-analysed psychoanalyst, all traces of longing for a narcissistic return have been successfully sublimated. On the other hand, he heads an international movement, he plans and schemes, explores and writes, works unstoppably; something drives him on. In fact, Freud's ambitious consciousness of his own worth and his desire to make his mark on society seem to have been major determinants of his creative energy, as significant as his awareness of the intrinsic importance of what he was doing. Freud was no retiring scientist, sheltering behind his obscurity in order to find the freedom to pursue his vocation. Quite the contrary: he went to considerable pains to ensure the propagation of his own ideas, through his own organisation and preferred acolytes. He acted, in the sense shared by all artists, in such a way as to defy death, continually producing books, analysing patients, writing and re-writing articles, thus promoting the preservation of his name. If this is not narcissism, what is? But if it is narcissism, does it reduce to a longing for unity and absorption in the other, a longing to return to the womb?

There are two important issues here: first, the extent to which the regressive longings of the ego for its undifferentiated state can be productive of positive states of mind and of creative activity; secondly, the extent to which all forms of narcissism can be understood in these regressive terms. Freud's general attitude is to repudiate anything which seems mystical and unbounded; despite his utilisation of literary sources, he is unpoetic in intention. Yet he is aware and deeply appreciative of creativity, his own and that of others, particularly the great classical and romantic writers and visual artists. He understands this creativity to have its origins in unconscious, predominantly sexual desires: sublimation, the mental process behind creativity, is usually defined as the expression of a sexual impulse in a non-sexual and socially valued way (e.g. Laplanche and Pontalis, 1973, p. 431). In this understanding, what is creative always has its origins in the drive of Eros, the search for new ways of being, new links, new modes of expression and unification. It is a forward-looking process, a generative one, and is thus opposed to the regressive longings characterised by narcissistic withdrawal. If it is narcissism, it appears to be of a different kind from the womb-pursuit of the oceanic feeling. However, as in all of psychoanalysis, the story is never so simple and one-sided. According to an unchanging tenet of Freudian psychology, the purpose of a drive, its aim, is to achieve satisfaction, and satisfaction is defined as the reduction of tension, the return to a state of rest. This is as true of the sexual, life-enhancing drives of Eros as it is of its opposite; indeed, the expression of sexual urges is taken by Freud as the paradigm case for his tension-reduction model. But if creativity is sublimated sexuality, then the search for the new is not a rejection of the womb, but a hunt for better ways of returning to it – a search for new modes of drive-satisfaction, new, possibly more elaborate and complex, ways of returning to rest. In this reading, creativity is indeed narcissism and narcissism – like everything else – does indeed have the character of a return: behind the search for new expressions and objects, behind creativity and Eros, is the old longing for sleep.

In the dark aftermath of the First World War, Freud formulated the ultimate principle of return as the death drive. In 1914, however, in 'On Narcissism', Freud sees the narcissistic return as a search for unification with the other. There is no hint of death here, though much of nostalgia: 'To be their own ideal once more, in regard to sexual no less than other trends, as they were in childhood – this is what people strive to attain as their happiness' (1914, p. 95). Something idealising is present in this view of the childhood state, that 'primary narcissism', which is phantasised as the place in which all that is lost can be put right. Essentially, Freud is shifting from an understanding of happiness as the relatively straightforward, if always temporary, satisfaction of a drive, to a more complex idea of a search for something which once was present but now is lost – a holy grail vision of childhood paradise. Implicit in this is a stream in Freud's work that subtly opposes his primary affiliation to drive theory. Where drive theory emphasises the tension-reduction cycle within each individual, narcissism, read as a pilgrimage back to the phantasised past unity with the mother, is an aspect of object relations; that is, it theorises relationships with other people as having a formative influence on individual development. The sophistication of Freud's vision here lies in his understanding of how the ego develops through a process of internalisation of lost relationships with desired objects – an understanding which has proved paradigmatic for those psychoanalysts more wedded to object- than to drive-formulations of development. Intimately connected with this, however, is a further question that returns us to the wider cultural issues raised by narcissistic states. Why should there be such a desire for return, what is it about development that leads to it being experienced as a series of losses to be dealt with – a series of alienations – rather than as a sequence of new gains? Is this the nature of 'reality', or is it something to do with only certain sets of object relations, certain kinds of 'environmental failure'? And, consequently, to what extent is the search for the lost unity of ego and object, the idealisation of primary narcissism, a basic fact of human existence, rather than the product of specific conditions – modern conditions of personal and social fragmentation?

The ego ideal

Much of Freud's thinking on regressive narcissism is connected with the ego ideal, a notion which has become central in explorations of the relationships between narcissism on the one hand and, on the other, pathology, normality and creativity. Freud (1914) places the ego ideal in the context of the trajectory of ego development, from unity to separation accompanied by the pursuit of the lost utopia – or nirvana.

> The development of the ego consists in a departure from primary narcissism and gives rise to a vigorous attempt to recover that state. This departure is brought about by means of the displacement of libido onto an ego ideal imposed from without; and satisfaction is brought about from fulfilling this ideal. (p. 95)

'To be their own ideal once more': what happens is that, faced with the separations induced by reality, the narcissism which was originally directed towards the ego is now displaced onto an internal representative of the idealised object. The ego, impoverished through its losses and experiences of dependence, replenishes its strength – the individual's 'self-regard' – by fulfilment of the ego ideal, that is, by living up to the idealised internal image of the object. It is here that links between sublimation and the ego ideal start to appear. Freud distinguishes carefully: 'sublimation describes something that has to do with the instinct and idealisation something to do with the object' (pp. 88–9) and it is the latter process which underpins the ego ideal. Indeed, 'A man who has exchanged his narcissism for homage to a high ego ideal has not necessarily on that account succeeded in sublimating his libidinal instincts' (p. 89). Nevertheless, what Freud suggests in the notion of the ego ideal is that, faced with expulsion from the early state of paradisial unity, humans internalise versions of the lost, desired object, which they idealise, pay 'homage' to, endeavour to satisfy by living up to its demands. This must almost always involve repression of drive desires, but may also entail sublimation – the conversion of what is unacceptable into what is recognised as beautiful and good.

The description of the ego ideal in 'On Narcissism' is confusing partly because it predates the notion of the super-ego. With the advent of the revised structural theory of the mind in 'The Ego and the Id', it becomes clear that the 'modification of the ego' which takes place as a consequence of the Oedipus complex has a number of attributes, some idealising in the manner described above, others punitive and aggressive – introjections of the phantasised aggression of the castrating father and (in Freud's 1930 formulation) of the projected aggression towards the father felt by the boy himself. (The complications of the Oedipus complex in girls, specifically that it is initiated rather than completed by the castration complex, results, according to Freud, in the rather weak super-egos of women – see Frosh (1987) for a discussion of this.) But at this point Freud does not distinguish between super-ego and ego-ideal; he uses the terms interchangeably to convey the notion of this mental structure built up from internalisations of the parental/paternal image. What is confusing here is that the similarity of process – setting up in the mind an internalised representation of an external object – masks a difference of content. The ego ideal was originally employed to describe a strategy for recovering the lost narcissism of early infancy; the super-ego is quite clearly an agency set up at the time of the stunning repressions that close the Oedipus complex – as a mode of identification with the aggressor. The former concept refers to a desire for absorption in the I-thou unboundedness of the first two-person relationship – the absorption of self in other – whereas the latter is linked to the three-person definitiveness of culture and reality, the 'ego-other-Law' mode of what Lacanians refer to as the Symbolic. The significance of this is to make it clear that the pursuit of oneness, of narcissistic nirvana, of the ego ideal, is the pursuit of the pre-Oedipal relationship, the time when there was not only no father, but no structure either, no *mediation* between the untrammelled desire of the infant and the illimitable response of the mother. Thus, this is a regressive pursuit of the presocial time before desire becomes structured, before incest can be recognised as such, before even self and other are distinguished – let alone the social structures that fix them along particular axes or inside specific discourses. The super-ego, however, embodies sets of restrictions, boundaries and identifications which are part of these social structures – the indices of an organisation through which sexuality reaches its mature form. In a nutshell, the ego-ideal represents escapist imagination, the super-ego reality.

The most trenchant expositor of this view of the ego ideal is the French psychoanalyst, Janine Chasseguet-Smirgel (1975, 1984). Following Freud closely, she sees the ego ideal not so much as something given from outside, but as the carrier of the subject's own narcissism, created as a projection from the ego in the moment when the first object relations are formed. This moment is the one in which the infant begins to perceive its weakness, becomes aware that the omnipotence which its link to the mother gave it was only a phantasy, something which belonged outside – and now the world has ravaging as well as nurturing possibilities, and the child is shut off from the source of its power. This moment has calamitous and also initiating consequences:

> The violent end to which the primary state of fusion is brought by [the infant's] helplessness obliges the infant to recognise the 'not-me'. This seems to be the crucial moment when the narcissistic omnipotence that he is forced to give up is projected on to the object, the infant's first Ego Ideal, a

narcissistic omnipotence from which he is henceforth divided by a gulf that he will spend the rest of his life trying to bridge. (1975, pp. 6–7)

Lasch (1984) glosses this account in a manner demonstrating the links with widespread cultural aspirations: 'this original experience of overwhelming loss becomes the basis of all subsequent experience of alienation, of historical myths of a lost golden age, and of the myth of the primary fall from grace, which finds its way into so many religions'. In addition, however, it fuels a search for reunification which can become apparent in creative action as well as in simple regressive longing. Here, however, is the difficult issue: to distinguish between what is creative and what is regressive. Lasch (1984, p. 164), for example, makes a claim which would suit modernists in their critique of postmodernism, but which may not be sustainable in the quick hindsight of cultural criticism:

> What distinguishes contemporary art from the art of the past, at least from the art of the nineteenth and early twentieth centuries, is the attempt to restore the illusion of oneness without any acknowledgement of an intervening experience of separation.

Mindlessness is the accusation here: creativity, which is a process having something to do with the transformation of materials in the service of a struggle to re-imagine reality, is replaced by nostalgia, by oceanic experiences and trance-inducing imagery which, to employ a psychoanalytic metaphor, have more to do with hypnosis than working through. For this is the crux of the argument: creativity, like mental health in general, is concerned with facing reality, with acting upon it, transforming it, expressing, repairing, regenerating it and the emotions it produces. Narcissism, embedded structurally in the attempt of the ego to merge with the ego ideal, is the denial of difference in favour of an imagined land in which there is no separation and loss, no unmet desire and, indeed, no work. The ego ideal, even though it fulfils a reality-principle function by establishing the existence of plans and hopes (i.e. postponements of pleasure), holds out a seductive promise of return to the longed-for early state when ego and non-ego were merged; it is, therefore, more a carrier of regressive than of creative urges.

Chasseguet-Smirgel has her own, highly contentious, view of what is genuinely creative and what is not, a view connected with her ideas on 'perversion'. First, however, she makes the distinction between ego ideal and super-ego advanced above – between the heirs to narcissism and the Oedipus complex.

At a certain level, there exists a fundamental difference between the Ego Ideal, heir to primary narcissism, and the super-ego, heir to the Oedipus complex. The first represents – at the outset at least – an attempt at recovering lost omnipotence. The second, in a Freudian perspective, is a product of the castration complex. The first tends to reinstate Illusion, the second to promote reality. The super-ego comes between the child and the mother, the Ego Ideal . . . pushes him towards fusion. (1975, p. 76)

What is central here, as in the quotation from Lasch above, is the valuing of a certain approach to difference – of ability to tolerate the experience of one's own helplessness and dependence, of acceptance of loss and a striving to make good whatever flows from it. This only comes with the working through of the castration complex: the subsequent psychic reformulations enable the structuring realities of the social world to be appreciated and lived with, even if they have to beget repression and guilt. But it is not the ego ideal in itself which is regressive; rather, it is the pursuit of the ego ideal without the mediation of reality represented by the Oedipus complex – without, that is, acceptance of separation. The ego ideal actually offers the possibility of a creative striving which, being based on a search for the original mothering experience, can have a loving rather than a punitive aspect. In addition, the experience of loss that produces the ego ideal in the first place can set in train a series of movements towards more activity and greater psychological differentiation, including identifications with deeply loved internalised others.

What makes the ego ideal regressive is the denial of difference. The setting-up of the super-ego not only institutes the order of reality; it also relieves some of the pressure for immersion in the other and loss of boundary which the ego ideal imposes. For narcissism has its dangers as well as its attractions: as described earlier in this chapter, its very fascination with surfaces belies its inner emptiness; moreover, its abandonment of boundaries produces a terror of engulfment. The distinctions and proprieties implemented through the Oedipus complex allow relief from this; the self may not have the same possibility of reunification, but it also is in less danger of total dissolution.

Chasseguet-Smirgel argues that not only sexual difference, but also generational difference is crucial here.

> I consider that the bedrock of reality is not only the difference between the sexes, but that which corresponds absolutely to this, like the two faces of a coin: namely, the difference between the generations. The reality is not that the mother has been castrated; the reality is that she has a vagina that the little boy's penis cannot satisfy. The reality is that the father has a penis and prerogatives that are still only potentialities in the little boy. (1975, p. 15)

Denial of difference is, according to Chasseguet-Smirgel, at the heart of perversion; it is also present in the narcissistic disavowal of the castration complex, with its concomitant promise to the pre-Oedipal boy that he can be a perfect partner to the mother (who has a phallus and therefore needs no husband) and to the girl that she can have her baby with no paternal intervention, for there is no boundary to cause a separation of sexes or generations. For Chasseguet-Smirgel, this makes it impossible for the pervert to be truly creative; rather, the pervert's creativity is founded only on the narcissistic desire to return to the lost, illusory state of unity; true creativity requires a grappling with difference, with the reality of the father. Aware of their lack of true identity, these perverts endeavour to create; but what they make will not have the truly transmuted quality of genuine creativity.

Nobody's son, the person I am describing, cannot 'father' an authentic work, drawing his life force from a rich and full libido. The identity that he assumes will necessarily be usurped since it will be based on a denial of his lineage. The symbolic phallus created in this way cannot but be itself factitious, that is to say a 'fetish'. (1975, p. 102)

Idealisation is linked to fakery; authentic creativity requires sublimation.

The real father

Chasseguet-Smirgel's emphasis on the disjunction between perversion and creativity has been powerfully criticised for its over-generalisations and a priori judgements on the quality of work produced by so-called 'perverts', particularly homosexuals (see, for example, Cunningham, 1986). However, her elucidation of the nature and regressive tendencies of the ego ideal are helpful in attempts to understand the phenomena of narcissism. There is general acceptance amongst psychoanalysts of the existence of some state of 'primary narcissism' (see Chapter 4); much that passes for activity in the contemporary world is an expression of a longing for return to this fantasised blissful state. In terms of psychic structure, this longing is institutionalised in the ego ideal, the internalised representation of the early lost object. But it is not the process of internalisation which is in itself problematic, for internalisation, as discussed earlier, is the characteristic way in which the ego develops. What is damaging is when internalised regressive longings fail to be tempered by recognition of reality. Psychoanalytically, this can be placed in the arena of the father, the symbolic matrix of the Oedipus complex. Without some exposure to this matrix and acceptance of its limits, sexual and generational boundaries dissolve and the ego is left to be absorbed back into the object; no longer is there a self with an integrity and boundary of its own. Moreover, according to Chasseguet-Smirgel, there is a political danger in the non-recognition of the father that is implied in the pursuit of the ego ideal, a danger recognisable in the tyranny of leaders over groups.

> (The) leader is not the father's substitute; on the contrary, he is the man who implicitly promises the coming of a world without any father and a correlative union with the almighty mother, the one before the breaking up of primary fusion, even with the one before birth. (1984, p. 61)

Groups, that is 'thirst less after a leader than after illusions' (ibid.).

Béla Grunberger, in a long series of papers (e.g. 1979, 1989), has supplied the most trenchant available critique of regressive narcissism. Grunberger (1989) locates the origins of narcissism in the pre-natal state of the foetus, which he refers to as 'prenatal coenesthesis' – a perfect state of holistic completeness. This state, phantasised later as non-instinctual, indeed non-physiological, is the source of all the sensations of regressive narcissism, sensations which derive their powerful positive pull from the fact that their actual illusoriness is rooted in an earlier condition in which they were the truth of the subject's existence.

> All the psychic peculiarities we habitually ascribe to man and which he cathects in a supremely narcissistic mode – completeness, omnipotence, an awareness of his own special worth, the exultant tendency to expansion, serenity, the feeling of freedom and autonomy, absolute independence, invulnerability, infinity and purity – derive directly from the prenatal coenesthesis experienced by the foetus. (p. xii)

The prenatal state of bliss is lost at birth, but it remains a reminiscence, at first inchoate, then becoming, through a process of 'deferred action', an unconscious position opposing that other great dimension of psychological existence, the drives. For Grunberger, development consists of an uneasy dialectic of narcissism and drive, in which the main task is to forge an integrative 'double process of narcissising ("egotis-ing") the drives (through the integration of conflict) and of integrating narcissism into instinctual maturation, and eventually into the ego' (p. 186), a task which may later become an aspect of psychoanalytic treatment.

At birth, however, there is a long way to go before the infant can cope with the loss of the primal state of unity with the mother and exposure to the demands and potential lack of fulfilment of her or his own drives. Much as in many object relations theories (and he makes an explicit reference to 'transitional objects' here), Grunberger's account emphasises the supportive, unifying role of the mother, who re-creates the prenatal environment by offering the infant a special, all-inclusive relationship that protects her or him from the demands of both the external world and the internal drives. This special relationship, recreated in part in psychoanalysis, is called by Grunberger 'the monad',

> The monad is a nonmaterial womb which functions as though it were material; on the one hand, it encloses the child in its narcissistic universe; on the other, it prepares it for the partial dissolution of that universe – or, in other words, for the dissolution of its own essence. (p. 3)

The monad protects and reassures the child by recreating the womb-experience, but it also makes it possible for the drives to begin to operate without the infant being overwhelmed by the unmasterable designs of reality. For this seems to be the major purpose of the drives in Grunberger's account: to urge the infant to 'master the real' (p. 12). The monad allows the infant to be eased into this task, rather than be crushed by the devastating loss it entails; the inevitable failures of the monad – the frustrations and separations experienced by the infant – gradually mobilise the drives and lead to a revaluation of the mother as a real object, towards whom desire can be directed. However, given the agonies of both world and drives, coupled with the regressive pull of the prenatal Eden, descent into narcissism is a permanent and pervasive human tendency.

> Given that it is part of his subjective reality, man will go on demanding to return to the ideal state he experienced in the womb and which, for a while and in a sense, he continued to experience in the monad. (p. 12)

It will be clear that Grunberger presents an opposition between narcissism and the drives: the two enter into a crucial relationship with one another that determines the outcome of the developmental process, but they are separable, they are alternative principles or dimensions, resulting in a crucial and unavoidable ambiguity within each individual human subject. However, he does not see the two dimensions as possessing equal value. Despite his appreciation of the necessity of narcissism and his sympathetic picture of the roots of regressive desire in the reality of the foetal experience, Grunberger quite clearly sides with the drives and with what he represents to be their affiliation with reality. This leads him to some startling insights into the nature of 'purity' and anality, insights that produce a very clear account of the links between idealisation and oppression. For Grunberger, the apparently spiritual pursuit of purity is an attempt to recover the narcissistic fantasy of wholeness, of a time before desire, before the spoiling ravages of the drives. Purity is opposed to anality – to the reality of dirt and the dirt of reality. Purity is what ideologues seek for, what people kill one another for: the preservation of their own image of the unspoilt maternal essence, at all costs. Purity is, therefore, a direct expression of regressive narcissism.

> Primary narcissism has a tendency to go on existing in the form of an ideal of absolute purity, as does the primitive fiction of being able to achieve narcissistic completeness by means which are completely divorced from corporeal factors, and without having to turn for help to oedipal psychosexual evolution: purity can, therefore, be defined as a narcissistic ideal of omnipotence and absolute sovereignty (well-being) that is completely free from the instinctual dimension. (p. 91)

The introduction of the 'instinctual dimension' requires an encounter with anality, with acknowledgement of the existence of conflict, struggle, doubt – all central components of a reality characterised by ambivalence and messy contradiction. This is why Grunberger opposes narcissism with anality, claiming, 'the triumph of narcissism over anality means not only an apparent liberation from Oedipus and from conflict, but also a liberation from reality – or, in a phrase, from the human condition' (p. 155). Anality is therefore a crucial element in development; moreover, the encounter with anality marks the division between narcissistic regression and Oedipal progression, tendencies which Grunberger assimilates both to a pathology/health opposition and to one between maternal and paternal principles.

Grunberger views the Oedipus as a transcendence of primary narcissism, in line with reality.

Since the child is condemned to leave his cocoon and to integrate himself into the world, he must acquire a new existential dimension based on drives, on castration, and on the defences against them. Henceforth frustration and narcissistic mutilation will be his daily bread. This whole maturational process is orientated towards the Oedipus . . . Where narcissism was, there Oedipus will be. (p. 34)

To some extent, Oedipal conflicts can be narcissistically informed, in that the construction of an external constraint on action is experienced by the infant as less demoralising than the appreciation of narcissistic failure – the father's power is a better excuse for failure to conquer the mother than is acknowledgement of the child's own sexual insufficiency. However, the true, full Oedipus complex is a confrontation with reality, with the individual's inability to make from it a perfectly pure and conflict-free arena of blissful passivity. Refusal to face the Oedipus is the principal characteristic of the narcissist; this is what makes the narcissistic search for perfection – for the ego ideal – so regressive. Narcissists deny the Oedipus and with it they deny the possibility for change; hence, they also deny the existence of anything or anyone outside themselves, and they refuse to identify with any external object. Grunberger's argument here forms the basis for Chasseguet-Smirgel's account of the pervert's denial of difference, for this is what all refusals of the Oedipus amount to: a failure to tolerate otherness that can lead to a desire to obliterate the other. In Oedipal terms, this means the refusal to recognise the existence of the father.

The Oedipal person reacts to failure as a stimulus to attempt the fulfilment of his Oedipal wishes with renewed determination, but for the narcissist there is no next time, since he prefers the disappearance of the system in which the injury took place . . . He will not try to triumph over the father (to identify with him in order to surpass him later) but will try to abolish the principle of paternity itself and the whole frame of reference of which it was the organiser. (p. 39)

Narcissism is regressive because it prefers the imaginary over the real; in Grunberger's terms , it remains in the realm of the maternal, of fantasy, refusing to struggle with the paternal principle that marks the acceptance of the drives and the appearance of real external power.

Grunberger's ambivalence towards the maternal dimension is very striking. On the one hand, he suggests that it offers, through the formation of the monad, protection to the new-born infant as she or he struggles with the demands of the drives and of external reality. In this sense, the first regressive, narcissistic solution is an essential precursor to healthy development. On the other hand, the maternal is imagined as the source of all denials of reality, and consequently as the origin of the narcissistic-aggressive impulse to destroy those who threaten the purity of existence – to destroy everyone with whom, and everything with which, the narcissist comes into conflict. The maternal is consequently seen not just as regressive, but as potentially destructive: too strong and all-embracing a monad results in obliteration of the other. As an alternative to this, the Oedipus complex, with its stress on the activity of paternal constraint, provides an opportunity to come to grips with the real – with otherness, discord, restriction, frustration – in such a way that the child identifies with the other and therefore internalises the possibilities for growth. Rather than adopt the criticisms of the patriarchal Oedipus-fixation of psychoanalysis employed by many modern critics, particularly feminists, Grunberger asserts that there is no other way for psychoanalysis, that 'psychoanalysis lives or dies by the Oedipus' (1989, p. 176). Denial of the Oedipus, denial of the paternal principle, means a dangerous immersion in the mother – an immersion in the sensuality of purity, oneness, passivity, phantasy. A question which arises here, of course, is to what extent this idea of Grunberger's is itself a denial of the challenge and difference introduced into psycho-analysis by those who confront its Oedipal fixation.

Grunberger makes some powerful links between his analysis of primary narcissism and a wider critique of totalitarian processes and ideological narcissistic-regressive solutions to internal conflicts – notably antisemitism. On a more general cultural level, Lasch (1984) argues for a literal reading of the purported link between narcissistic personality structures and modern family life in terms based largely on those employed by Chasseguet-Smirgel and Grunberger: specifically, the absence or weakness of the father is held to accentuate the unbridled plunge into phantasies of Oedipal triumph and solipsistic control. More poignantly, however, Lasch also draws attention to the way general principles of stability, boundary and permanence are undermined in modern western culture, weakening the superego and strengthening the role of the ego ideal and the search for lost illusions.

> The culture of narcissism is not necessarily a culture in which moral constraints on selfishness have collapsed or in which people released from the bonds of social obligation have lost themselves in a riot of hedonistic self-indulgence. What has weakened is not so much the structure of moral obligations and commandments as the belief in a world that survives its inhabitants. (p. 193)

With no experience of the stability of the external world, the internal one runs rife with phantasies of reunion and resurrection; with no comprehension of time or depth, all things become interchangeable – present, future, past; mother, father, child; self and other. It is this insight which is the progressive element in the rather troubling assimilation of mothering to regression which can be found in the work of these theorists. Narcissism represents a retreat from reality into a phantasy world in which there are no boundaries; this can be symbolised by the early monad, in which the mother offers the new-born infant an extended period of self-absorption and limitless, omnipotent contentment. Using the terminology of maternity here draws attention to the way this is a pre-Oedipal state in which the infant recognises nothing outside her- or himself because of the supportive ministrations of the mother. However, employment of the terminology of maternity can lead to a disparagement of mothering as in itself a regressive process – a tendency which does seem to be present in Grunberger's work in particular. The point should not be to oppose mothering with fathering: the assimilation of these terms to a regression/progression dichotomy is precisely one of the most pervasive forms of patriarchal misogyny, and can perhaps be interpreted as fear of femininity arising out of a terror of dissolution as established structures give way. Instead, Grunberger's important opposition between narcissism and Oedipus can be employed without the feminine/masculine overtone. Narcissism is the regressive tendency, absorption in the oneness which was once the foetal and infantile experience of the mother, but which is more generally a refusal to engage with reality. Its consequence is a mixture of terrified withdrawal into an imaginary arena, and violent obliteration of otherness. Oedipus, the recognition of and grappling with the power of the external world, may be painful in its enforcement of structure on limitless desire, but it can be more painful still to live in the disappearing void of complete self-annihilation.

Chapter 4

Narcissistic Pathology

Narcissism and society

The search for reunion, however illusory it may be, is linked to the narcissistic experience of emptiness in relationships and, more brutally, in the self. Thus, it is in part a response to the partially glimpsed reality of psychological impoverishment in contemporary culture; it may be an imaginary world to which we strive to return, but this world does at least mark out a sphere of difference – of potential 'betterness' – against which the barrenness of narcissism can be calibrated. In short, there is an element of healthy longing in the desire for return, even if the solution is a false one – denial rather than working through. The ego ideal, slippery and unrealistic though it may be, has its starting point in the internalisation of a loved lost object, a sense of what is possible, of what true connectedness might be.

Margaret Mahler's version of what Winnicott calls primary maternal preoccupation, and what Grunberger terms the monad, acts as a leitmotif in many psychoanalytic accounts of narcissistic pathology. Mahler (e.g. Mahler *et al*, 1975) focuses on *individuation* as the dominating axis of early development: a natural process of separating out and becoming an independent being. The starting point for this development is a moment of blissful merger marked by awareness of impending change, a moment of symbiosis with the mother.

In psychoanalytic developmental psychology, the symbiotic phase marks the beginning of object relations, with the dawning awareness of mother's ministrations along with the dawning awareness of the self that is gratified. This sense of

95

blissful unity with the loved one is what is sought in the consummation of sexual love. This omnipotent gratification of all needs, including complete autonomy, is what the so-called narcissistic personality seeks in unconscious fantasies of retaining this self-object state. And this is the merger of self and object representations to which the ego regresses in the borderline conditions and in psychosis, with varying degrees of severity. (White, 1980, p. 148)

The continuing lure of narcissism derives from the difficulties created by the delayed 'psychological birth' of the human infant, whose selfhood is always exposed to the risks of swamping fusion or devastating isolation. The whole of the life cycle, suggests Bromberg (1982), can be seen as 'a more or less successful distancing from, and introjection of, the lost symbiotic mother' (p. 442), with an eternal longing for an ideal state of self which in fact is a phantasised re-absorption into the symbiotic state. Such a regression, as White points out, represents a loss of self-other boundaries of a kind more characteristic of psychotic than narcissistic states, but it is widely understood as one underlying danger against which narcissistic symptomatology defends.

Building on this in a slightly different way, several psycho-analytic theorists, to some extent following Freud's link between narcissistic libido and sublimation, suggest that some narcissism is healthy, necessary, for example, for creativity, empathy with others, acceptance of death. This stresses the positive value of the initial symbiotic link between infant and mother, in which the self is experienced as part of something larger, as not distinguished from the other. Such an exper-ience, it is suggested, provides a necessarily omnipotent basis for a strong sense of self-worth and potential and is also a prototype for the more lasting ability to 'get inside another's skin', to understand, emotionally as well as intellectually, what the world is like from another's point of view and to feel at one with them. This makes sense of the idea that narcissism and empathy can go together: 'the groundwork for our ability to obtain access to another person's mind is laid by the fact that in our earliest mental organisation the feelings, actions and behaviour of the mother had been included in our self' (Kohut, 1966, p. 78). Similarly, the primary identification with the mother is said to lay the basis for an expansion of self late in life as a way of coping with the impending dissolution of death – a view apparently in opposition to Lasch's (1984) argument that narcissists, unable to deal with the self-other boundaries of reality, are also unable to face the boundedness of death. The positive rendering of primary narcissism is reminiscent of Freud's 'Principle of Constancy', later developed into the notion of the death drive: that all living things strive to 'return' to a state of non-being, to a restful and undisturbed, even inorganic, absorption into a wider totality. This vision of life as an unfortunate interruption in an eternal blissful sleep may not have much neurology to recommend it (the nervous system does not, in fact, strive for rest, but is endlessly active, with changes being in the pattern more than the quantity of activation), but it does make a certain degree of poetic sense of the fairly widespread search for escape from contemporary urban culture. Phantasies of rural peace, of desert island solitude, of transcendence; these have to do both with narcissism and with death.

It is not, however, the normality of the narcissistic phase which is concentrated on in the aetiological theories of narcissistic pathology, but disturbances in this phase, particularly in fulfilling the grandiose needs of the developing self. For Mahler, it seems to be that the infant's natural enjoyment of her or his growing independence is supported by a facilitating mother, who makes it possible for the 'psychological birth' of the child to occur within a context of loving support. The more familiar version of this, present in object relations theory in particular, is that it is the necessary failures of the mother to completely meet all the infant's demands that forces the formation (or recognition) of a self-other boundary. What matters, in Winnicottian and related approaches, is that the mother should fail the child from within a context in which the infant's early grandiose needs have been met sufficiently for a strong inner core of self to have been formed. This allows the child to withstand the frustrations of separation, of having needs which are not quite met; 'optimal frustration' is the optimal phrase. If the mother fails the child too early, the self will never be formed, or will be hidden away behind a mask; if she fails too late, or too suddenly, the boundaries of selfhood will always be confused – grandiose, but insecure.

Primary narcissism, unity of self and other, is a state which cannot be sustained: an impossible phantasy, doomed to be broken by the realities of human existence. What matters for the development of narcissistic character pathology are the conditions under which this fracturing occurs. On this point most commentators agree, whatever their views on the content of the narcissistic condition. It is the mode of failure of the interpersonal setting that dictates the extent of health or pathology in the self system as it forms from the self-other symbiosis. Narcissism arises as a product of the environment's – universally in these theories, the mother's – failures to recognise and respond appropriately to the needs of the infantile self. At the source of this failure, all agree, are the unmet narcissistic needs of the mothers themselves, their own inability to form full relationships with their infants which are based on an empathic understanding of the child's need state, and not of their own. Thus, for example, Kernberg (1970, p. 220) suggests that a frequent feature of the background of narcissistic patients involves a 'chronically cold parental figure with covert but intense aggression'. He goes on to describe the typical ('composite') patient as having 'a parental figure, usually the mother or a mother surrogate, who functions well on the surface in a superficially well-organised home, but with a degree of callousness, indifference, and non-verbalised, spiteful aggression'. The child of such a parent tries to win her love through some kind of achievement, that is, through living in accord with the mother's desire rather than his or her own. Especially if such children actually possesses some brilliant streak, they become – they have to become – special. But underlying this glitter is an extreme fear of dependence, because if they become dependent they are available to a repetition of the deep maternal rejection which they have already experienced.

Miller (1979b) makes a more formal intergenerational link here. She sees narcissistic disturbance as arising when the mother 'tries to assuage her own narcissistic needs through her child, i.e. she cathects him *narcissistically*' (p. 52). This does not mean that the mother does not love her child: 'On the contrary, the mother often loves her child as her self-object, passionately, but not in the way he needs to be loved.' The consequence of this for the child, desperately seeking after nurture and anxious to retain the parent's love, is that 'he develops something the mother needs, and this certainly saves his life (the mother's or the father's love) at the time, but it nevertheless may prevent him, throughout his life, from being himself' (ibid.). And here is the cause of this maternal dysfunction:

> With two exceptions, the mothers of all my patients had a narcissistic disturbance, were extremely insecure, and often suffered from depression . . . What these mothers had once failed to find in their own mothers they were able to find in their children: someone at their disposal who can be used as an echo, who can be controlled, is completely centred on them, will never desert them, and offers full attention and admiration. (p. 53)

The child as object, repeated through history. Children need parents to love them for what they are, not what they represent; internalisation of the failure to receive such love leads to a continuing inner emptiness and aching need, accompanied by a surface shallowness employed to ward off any who might come too close, reawaken the memory of infantile dependence, and resurrect the despair and rage behind. Given children of their own, such people, faced with the intensity of a child's demands, repudiate them in the same way in which they themselves were repudiated: they see in the child only what can reflect their own glory, only what can support their fragile selves – the child is truly only a narcissistic echo. And so, in Miller's account, it goes on: the failure of adults to respect children for what they are, for their own needs and demands, leads to these children becoming parents who are themselves unable to respect their children; walls are built up against true intimacy; conformity and inauthenticity – Winnicott's 'false self' – become the way of the world.

Kovel (1988, p. 197) supplies a wider social resonance to this personal and interpersonal failing:

> The child was regarded as an adornment of the parents, rather than a creature in her/his own right; and this parental concern had the quality of capital invested for a future yield.

The economic reductionism here is too deterministic, perhaps, but, in cartoon form at least, it indicates the extent of penetration of psychic life by narcissistic culture. The narcissistic parent carries the distress of the culture in which she or he is embedded, then replicates this state of affairs through distorted treatment of the child – through relating to the child as a commodity or as a mirror – producing another narcissistic personality. This is a consequence of social experience at two levels: the interpersonal origins of the parent's own inner impoverishment, as described by Miller, and the wider characteristics of modern culture, of late capitalism. There, the concern is with people as commodities and with 'investment' in a child for the future benefits – social legitimation or economic support – which she or he might bring. Moreover, in contrast to other forms of social organisation which also regard children (at least sons) as forms of economic investment, modern western culture overinvests in them psychologically whilst also treating them in a commodity form. This is to be seen in the marketing strategies used to construct children as consumers: a child has to be gratified, must never be thwarted, or she or he will feel 'deprived', but this gratification is translated solely into material terms. That is, consumption no longer *symbolises* care and affection, the gift no longer *represents* underlying love; it *is* the whole of love, the way in which intimacy is negotiated. In postmodern culture, the deepest needs of children are no longer meetable without translation into material form – translation and trivialisation at the same time. As people become interchangeable, as their lives become losing battles for a sense of location and roots, they can do less and less for their children, who are asking, more poignantly and desperately and urgently, for exactly the same things.

Selfobjects and mirrors

Kohut articulates many of these ideas with considerable power and with a focus on the development of the 'self' as an active centre of psychological experience that links him with humanistic as well as psychoanalytic thinkers. For Kohut, narcissism is a normal developmental phase and the grandiose and idealising tendencies that inform narcissism have a respectable place in every infant's life. However, when these tendencies are not negotiated successfully, the self grows in a distorted or partial way, stuck in part or whole at the infant phase. And this is an interpersonal issue: the self is forged in the furnace of early relationships with others; it is when these do not provide it with the developmental supports it needs, that it comes out lop-sided or melted away.

In the beginning of interpersonal relationships, in Kohut's account, is a kind of absorption of others into the schema of the self. The child's own self is too fragile to survive on its own; in Greenberg and Mitchell's (1983) gloss, 'it requires the participation of others to provide a sense of cohesion, constancy and resilience' (p. 353). This participation comes by way of contributions from the child's parents, who support the incipient selfhood of the child as if they were not separate people at all, but part of the child's own psychic structure. That is, the infant relies on these outside objects, the parents, to maintain the integrity of her or his inner world; they *are* the scaffolding for the self. Because of their inextricable immanence within the child's subjectivity, Kohut names the formative objects 'selfobjects', describing them as 'objects which we experienced as part of ourself; the expected control over them is, therefore, closer to the concept of the control which a grown-up expects to have over his own body and mind than to the concept of the control which he expects to have over others' (Kohut and Wolf, 1978, p. 177). This notion reflects a more refined conceptualisation of the positive potential of primary narcissism: being at one with the object is not necessarily escapist, but can represent a way of taking in the goodness of that object and deriving from it workable boundaries and supports for the self. It is also, as Greenberg and Mitchell (1983, p. 353) point out, a mode of empathy with a self-reflexive component: 'in the child's merger with his selfobjects, there is a subtle yet pervasive participation in the adult's experience, including the adult's experience of the child'.

In early life there are two types of selfobject: 'those who respond to and confirm the child's innate sense of vigour, greatness and perfection; and those to whom the child can look up and with whom he can merge as an image of calmness, infallibility and omnipotence' (Kohut and Wolf, 1978, p. 177) – the 'mirroring selfobject' and 'idealised parental imago', respectively. The successful internalisation of these two self-objects can be seen as two chances for the consolidation of the self, relating 'to the establishment of the child's cohesive grandiose-exhibitionist self (via his relation to the empathic-ally responding merging-mirroring-approving selfobject) on the one hand, and to the establishment of the child's cohesive idealised parent-imago (via his relation to the empathically responding selfobject parent who permits and indeed enjoys the child's idealisation of him and merger with him) on the other' (Kohut, 1977, p. 185). These two chances occur at different times: grandiosity and omnipotence are rooted in the earliest 'symbiotic' absorption in the mother, whereas idealisa-tion and identification are more akin to somewhat later, perhaps Oedipal, interpersonal structures. But the main point is that the two chances are genuine: either kind of selfobject can lay the foundations for a healthy self, although the exact nature of that self will vary depending on which it is and on what the history of both sets of selfobjects has been. Put extremely crudely, either maternal or paternal imago can help the child establish a self; failure of both, however, is a disaster.

If all goes well, the selfobjects are internalised so that the self has a strong core which then enables it to begin to appreciate the externality of others, and to relate to them in an empathic and meaningful way. In Kohutian terms, a process of 'transmuting internalisation' occurs in which the selfobjects become poles for the development of the self – a process which has similarities with Kleinian and object relational ideas of introjection of the object. If, however, the child is faced with disapproval and rejection from the early selfobjects, then the internal world never achieves the positive flavouring required for healthy development. Instead, the early narcissistic self is experienced as under attack, and its grandiose and idealising inclinations become repressed rather than realistically modified – leading to vacillations of the ego between irrational over-estimation of the self and feelings of inferiority (Kohut, 1966, pp. 68–9). Thus the exhibitionism and grandiosity of the child remain in action in a repressed form, unrealistic and unrealised in any healthy way, with failure and rejection experienced as deeply shameful and disturbing, and with chronic manipula-tiveness and avoidance of dependency the only possible paths to interpersonal stability. The failure to 'transmute' the selfobjects means that they are troublingly exciting but uncontrollable, always threatening to destroy the self which has been left without any stable basis for survival. This threat is of the grossest kind: it involves not guilt (which, Kohut notes, is the focus of much classical psychoanalytic theory), but dismantling of the self – annihilation. In consequence, the narcissist's struggle for continued being, the struggle against exposure to real dependency and intimacy and hence further rejection, is a life-and-death one, a desperate struggle for survival of the self.

Put simply, narcissistic pathology represents a fixation at early stages of narcissistic development, caused by the failure of the parental selfobjects to respond empathically to the infant's grandiose needs. Like Lasch, and indeed like Winnicott, Kohut (1977) traces the origins of this failure to social conditions, particularly breakdown in those family structures needed to support the mother sufficiently for her to be able to tolerate and empathise constructively with her infant's grand-iose needs. No great feat of imagination is required here: in a society in which everyone's selfhood is undermined by the rapidity of cultural, economic and technological change, by uncertainty over who controls what (accompanied by a sense that someone or something is in control of each of us), by fascination with fantasies centred on interchangeable images, and by a severing of roots and traditions in the context of an increasing sameness of culture – in such a society, it must become increasingly difficult to offer a stable and still point around which the personality of a child can be formed. The child, too, aware of the parent's unease, sense of emptiness and loss, will internalise as selfobjects things which are shifting and unstable and hence unable to provide a secure basis for the construction of a viable self. And so culture and the individual feed each other: social uncertainty produces individual disease; personal emptiness leaves one open to the fragmenting and demeaning impact of collective regression. Here, in the contrast between what seems possible in infancy and what actually happens, is the most poignant element in the differentiation between what psychoanalysts take to be the normal absorption of the infantile self in the other of the mother, and a failure of the mature individual to make any real links with others at all. Call this, perhaps, secondary narcissism, although it is not really so in Freud's sense of the libidinal cathexis of the self; it is more like an inability to genuinely love anything, whether self or other. Thus Kohut (1966, p. 63): 'the antithesis to narcissism is not the object relation but object love'.

Much of Kohut's description of the narcissistic process has become accepted currency in psychoanalytic thinking. However, his argument that pathological narcissism is the same kind of thing as ordinary narcissism, that it represents a fixation at an early stage of development, has come under fire, especially from Kernberg. The importance of this debate can be seen particularly in relation to therapy: if Kohut is right, then the task of the analyst is to provide conditions mimicking those which earlier in life would have allowed healthy development to occur; if Kernberg is correct, then something else is required. This will be returned to later, although it is worth noting how this controversy resonates with wider disagreements in the analytic field about the conditions for therapeutic change, for example between object relations therapists and Kleinians (Frosh, 1987). For the moment, the necessity is to consider the case which Kernberg makes for differentiating between infantile narcissism and narcissistic pathology, a case based on five main grounds. These are: (i) the grandiose fantasies of normal children are more realistic than those of narcissistic patients; (ii) children's over-reactions to criticism and their need to be the centre of attention coexist with genuine positive and dependent feelings; (iii) normal infantile narcissism is reflected in a child's demandingness over real needs; (iv) children's self-centredness is emotionally warm, whilst that of narcissistic patients is cold; and (v) 'the normal infantile narcissistic fantasies of power and wealth and beauty . . . do not imply an exclusive possession of all that is valuable and enviable in the world . . . but this is a character-istic fantasy of narcissistic personalities' (1974, pp. 253–4). In summary, children's narcissism is normally accompanied by positive relationships with others and by genuine, if erratic, feelings in an accepted context of dependency; narcissistic pathology is defined by the inability of the narcissist to deal with intimacy and emotional warmth, and to trust anyone else at all.

It would be possible, perhaps, to reconcile Kernberg's points with Kohut's position by arguing that it is not just stuckness at an earlier phase of development which is represented by fixation, but a problematic replaying of the 'hurt' elements of this phase. However, Kernberg (1974, pp. 252–3) goes further, presenting a reading of narcissistic pathology that returns us to the structural considerations present in Freud's work and has implications for therapy. In outline, Kernberg argues three things. First, pathological narcissism is different not only from infantile narcissism but also from ordinary adult narcissism, which may be seen, for instance, in positive self-presentations. Secondly, he suggests that 'pathological narciss-ism can only be understood in terms of the analysis of the vicissitudes of libidinal and aggressive drive derivatives', with oral conflicts predominating. As will be seen below, it is particularly aggressive drives which count here, although it is also worth noting that in his later work, Kernberg seems to shift more forcefully to an object relational than a drive-based approach (see Greenberg and Mitchell, 1983). Finally, this is Kernberg's critical point, differentiating his ideas clearly from those of Kohut: 'the structural characteristics of narcissistic personalities . . . are a consequence of the development of pathological (in contrast to normal) differentiation and integration of ego and super-ego structures, deriving from pathological (in contrast to normal) object relationships'. In striving to retain the notion of something distorted, not just restrained, Kernberg makes it necessary to think that, at the heart of a culture in which narcissism flourishes, there must be something terribly wrong.

The raging self

It is apparent from the complexity and subtlety of the descriptions of narcissism to be found in the work of Kohut, Kernberg and others, that the concept has moved a considerable way since Freud's early drive-based formulation which focussed on the redirection of libidinal energy away from external objects and onto the ego. In particular, something has entered into the psychoanalytic lexicon under the guise of the 'self', sometimes explicitly – as in Kohut's designation of his approach as 'self theory', or Winnicott's use of the terms 'true' and 'false self' to characterise healthy and conformist psychological structures – and sometimes less obviously. It almost certainly represents an improvement in the accessibility of psychoanalytic ideas when analysts refer to the 'self' rather than 'narcissistic cathexes': it makes the whole approach more human and humane, speaking the language of ordinary experience. So we are narcissists, and this means that there is something confused or conflicted in our selves; this is simple to say and understand. But even though ordinary language is less alienating than scientistic mystification (as Bettelheim (1983) points out in relation to the translations of Freud's work), it can nevertheless be deceptive, sometimes precisely because of its familiarity. Because we think we know what is meant by the 'self', we assume understanding of theories that employ it; because the self is so central to our thinking about our everyday experiences, we tend to accept the truth of approaches that make the self central to their own explanation of psychic phenomena. What is potentially misleading here is the same thing which is deceptive in any 'commonsense' account of experience – the same thing that encourages psychoanalysts to refuse to accept the statements and assumptions of their patients at face value. What seems obvious, commonsensical, humane, to be taken for granted, may be that which is most obfuscated by ideology – that which it is hardest to see through. If everyone shares the same illusion, the illusion is constantly confirmed and reinforced, becoming a universal assumption no longer in need of establishment. But it is an illusion nonetheless; the sun does not go round the earth, nor perhaps the earth around the self.

The self, then, is a contentious issue: does it exist or not; is it imaginary; what, if it does have substance, might it be? Kohut knows what he means by a healthy self. It has 'three major constituents':

(1) one pole from which emanate the basic strivings for power and success; (2) another pole that harbours the basic idealised goals; and (3) an intermediate area of basic talents and skills that are activated by the tension-arc that establishes itself between ambitions and ideals. (Kohut and Wolf, 1978, p. 177)

This description perhaps reveals the strong influence of American culture on psychoanalytic theories in its portrayal of the self as a mechanism for ambitions ameliorated by ideals, achieved through talents and skills. It certainly seems a long way from either the drive formulations of Freud or the relationship-oriented maps of selfhood offered by object relations theorists. Indeed, in some ways it appears to be more like the behaviourist 'self' which is the focus of assertiveness-training programmes. But this is simplifying Kohut's position too much. The relative health of this achieving self is determined by the quality of its interactions with its selfobjects in early childhood: a structurally unda-maged but 'stuck' self, still fixated on archaic grandiose self configurations and narcissistically-cathected objects, is at the source of narcissistic pathology. The fragility of the self and the failure of the environment (its selfobjects) to supply the conditions under which its infantile grandiosity could be validated and integrated into a stable source of realistic self esteem, means that external objects have to become the mechanisms for self-esteem regulation, resulting in the mirror-ing and exhibitionism which are diagnostic of narcissistic personalities. Narcissistic rage is a derivative of the weakness of the self: the desperation with which external validation is sought results in adult-infantile psychic tantrums when it is not obtained. White glosses: 'any real or imagined obstacle to such total control touches off a drop in self-esteem that is experienced as catastrophic . . . Narcissistic rage might be seen, then, as a primitive defence against acknowledging the limitations of oneself as a separate, imperfect being in a world of imperfect people' (1980, p. 154).

Thus, Kohut's claim is that the self has real existence, but is weak; it is the danger that the unintegrated and needy grandiosity of this self will be punctured that produces the patterns of narcissistic defence. This vision of personal needs emphasises validation (a human value present in most psychoanalytic theories) but it also paints a picture of adult selves as organised around self esteem. That is, all human activity is narcissistic in the sense that it is concerned with self-maintenance and with uncovering positive self-images; a culture structured around self reflections, mirrors and aggrandised exhibitionistic images, merely exaggerates what is fundamental in us all. All is presentational; feeling states are representations of the success or failure of self esteem regulation, interpersonal life is the stage on which this process is played out. In this respect, Kohut's theory suggests that the integrity of emotion has been undermined by its employment in the service of self image: where once there might have been indignation or righteous anger, there is now infantile tantrum; where there was sadness, there is now rage. And rage has changed: once it was a pure expression of slighted humanity; a Kohutian King Lear would have only empty bombast to his name. Is this contemporary western life or universal truth?

Rage is a central idea in Kernberg's version of narcissistic pathology. Where Kohut stresses the need of the impoverished grandiose self for support from its objects, and the rage which can result when this need is not met, Kernberg makes destructiveness more of a core phenomenon, arguing that narcissism is a defence against a rage which is pure and so full of hate that it threatens to completely destroy the vital nexus of self and other. Kernberg states that the deepest level of narcissistic pathology, is the image of a hungry, enraged, empty self, full of impotent anger at being frustrated, and fearful of a world which seems as hateful and revengeful as the patient himself. (1970, p. 219)

The failure of the early parenting environment to fulfil the infant's basic needs – or, in more Kleinian terms, to contain the infant's aggressive demands – leads to a deep and forceful oral rage, devaluing and devouring its objects in a dance of mutual persecution between inside and out. Narcissistic symptomatology is a defence against this rage, a means of holding the self together which is more effective than the strategies employed by borderline patients, whose inner fragmentation tends to be more severe. Narcissists are relatively successful, compared to these near-psychotic residents of the shadowy 'borderline' between sanity and insanity, because narcissistic defences are built on stronger-established ego boundaries and an integrated, if pathological, self – much as in Kohut's argument that narcissistic and borderline personalities are distinguished by the degree of establishment of the self, with the former being more secure. But there is no fundamental difference in kind. Just like borderlines, narcissists 'present a predominance of primitive defensive mechanisms such as splitting, denial, projective identification, omnipotence and primitive idealisation' whilst also showing 'the intense primitive quality of oral-aggressive conflicts characteristic of borderline patients' (Kernberg, 1970, p. 215). It is only their surface functioning which is superior; their underlying struggle is much the same. This is a Kleinian type of inner world, characterised by splitting and paranoid projections, with rage born of envy reined in only by a desperate defensive withdrawal from real relationships with others.

Kernberg offers a structural account of narcissism that portrays a disturbed and distorted self – not just a stunted one, as in Kohut's work. Severe oral deprivation in early life produces overwhelming aggression, managed through primitive defences, particularly splitting of self and object into idealised and denigrated parts. As in Klein's theory, such splitting serves the purpose of preventing the devastation of the residual loved and loving aspects of the personality by its more powerful destructive, envious aspects; through splitting, the idealised self and object can be kept relatively immune from its persecutory twin. But the price to be paid for the continued employment of this separation is, by definition, that it leads to a lack of integration and also to dissociation and 'alternating ego states in the perception both of the self and other people' (White, 1980, p. 159). The world fluctuates: paranoid and idealising, the narcissist's environment is haunted by spectres, continually changing their shape.

The grandiosity of the narcissist stems from the strategy adopted to overcome the painful splits produced by inner rage. This strategy involves fusing the ideal self, ideal object and actual self images together, producing an overvalued self which need not be dependent on others and therefore need fear neither rejection nor its own retributive violence. 'In their phantasies, these patients identify themselves with their own ideal self images in order to deny normal dependency on external objects and on the internalised representations of these external objects' (Kernberg, 1970, p. 217). Structurally,

> idealised object images which normally would be integrated into the ego ideal and, as such, into the super-ego, are condensed instead with the self concept. As a result, normal superego integration is lacking, ego-superego boundaries are blurred in certain areas, and unacceptable aspects of the real self are dissociated and/or repressed, in combination with widespread, devastating devaluation of external objects and their representations. (Kernberg, 1974, p. 262)

Experientially, the inner world of the narcissist has only the grandiose self, 'shadowy images' of self and others, persecutory super-ego forerunners, and 'primitive, distorted object images on to whom intense oral sadism has been projected' (ibid.). Thus, the shallow manipulativeness of narcissistic relationships, the absence of genuine feeling and the mirror-like superficiality of all involvement, is not due to an absence of emotion, but to too much feeling – to envy and rage, to overwhelming hatred and to aggression directed at the real defining absences of the narcissist's life.

Kernberg's description places the source of the narcissist's psychic pain in early experiences that result in an inner world structured around a split-off and repressed set of negative emotions or, more formally, ego-object relationships. Central to it, as in the Kleinian-style images described above, is the idea of an infant whose inner world, whose raw passions, cannot be fully experienced and tolerated by those around. That is, in the language of Bion, the parents are unable to sustain a state of reverie which would enable them to contain the infant's projections and make them safe; instead, they fear, deny, avoid or repudiate them. This means that the child's sense of her or his own destructiveness as being uncontrollable is confirmed by the environmental response to it, creating a feedback cycle in which inner rage is experienced as highly charged and dangerous, producing more splits and defences that aggravate the difficulties of self-integration, leaving rage to escalate as it is repeatedly unable to provoke a containing response. The desperate narcissistic and borderline defences are thenceforth all that stand between the self and its dissolution in the face of these unmet and uncontainable passions.

It is also a small step from here, though perhaps an even smaller step from Kohut's picture of the narcissistic self, to Winnicott's familiar true-self/false-self distinction, the former being the spontaneous representation of the individual's actual needs and desires, whilst the latter is a conforming, protective shell taken on as a protection against loss of love. The false self, in this sense, is an expression of the 'desire of the mother': it is an attempt to fit in, to anticipate the other's demands in order to maintain some kind of object relationship. But the object/other/mother has failed the child: unable to tolerate the infant's real demands, it ensures that artificial, appeasing ones are substituted in their place. In consequence, the child survives, but her or his needs are never really met. Miller (1979a) puts this in the context of narcissism:

> Whereas 'healthy narcissism' can be characterised as the full access to the true self, the narcissistic disturbance can be understood as a fixation on a 'false' or incomplete self . . . in order to maintain the object's love, these children developed

only those capacities which they felt their parents needed or admired. The unacceptable feelings had to be hidden from the environment and from themselves in order to avoid rejection or shame . . . If anger, envy, despair and other undesirable feelings cannot be avoided completely, they have to be split off and cannot be integrated, which leads to a marked impoverishment of the personality. (pp. 346–7)

Both the conformity and superficiality of the narcissistic false self and the underlying intolerable envy and aggression are recognised in this quotation. Miller argues that the grandiosity of the narcissist is related to depression and in turn to the intense 'psychotic' nature of childhood emotion. Kernberg, on the other hand, suggests that a central element in the psychopathology of narcissistic patients is an inability to feel depression – understood more or less as an inability to feel real – and that the extent to which this is the case is an important prognostic indicator. Both agree that if feeling explodes, the narcissist's phantasy is that self will explode as well.

There are disputes concerning the relationship between narcissistic, borderline, schizoid and psychotic states. These do not need to be dealt with here except to note that most theorists propose, explicitly or implicitly, gradations of severity in these disturbances, with narcissism being the mildest (though still potentially severe). More importantly, whatever distinctions are made, the theories of narcissism make it a form of pathology which is related to the other states in being organised around a set of defensive strategies having as their purpose the maintenance of the self. Kohut's approach suggests that a distinction between disturbances of self cohesion (as in borderline states) and self esteem (narcissism) may be useful; Kernberg's account shades narcissists in with borderlines by relating narcissism to disturbances in the structure of the self. All, however, present a picture of self development as a precarious achievement which occurs through absorption in an unreliable and potentially pathogenic set of interpersonal relationships. In a 'culture of narcissism', in which the interpersonal context is repeatedly destabilised and undermined, narcissists must consequently be reproduced.

Broken mirrors

The account above of the work of Kohut and Kernberg has
produced a view of narcissism as rooted in the failure of the
early social and parental environment to support the development of an integrated self, defined either in libidinal or in
object relational terms. The link between narcissistic pathology
and narcissistic parenting means that a culture that valorises
narcissism, or at least enmeshes its subjects in webs of
superficiality and glamorous but empty exteriors, will be
registered psychically and reproduced intergenerationally.
One cannot read off culture and politics automatically from
psychopathology, but when disturbances resonate with normal
functioning to the extent that narcissistic disturbances do, then
social organisation is likely to be at the core of both.
Commodity substitution and person replacement, literally
object exchange; everything is the same, only what glitters
can be mistaken for gold.

This resurrects an issue touched on earlier. The theorists of
narcissism, particularly the American theorists, may have
rather different ideas of what is meant by the term 'self', but
they are relatively untroubled by any worry that there may be
no such thing at all. Indeed, like most people, they see
meaning in the notion of a healthy or true self, as something
real, undoubtedly difficult to achieve, but having substance as
a psychic integration of genuine needs, experiences and desires.
The sense of self, striven for and held easily by many people,
felt to be uncomfortably precarious but nonetheless worth
preserving by others – this is an unproblematic entity in these
approaches, with narcissism and related disorders being what
emerges when the self threatens to disappear. As noted earlier,
this sense of something being an unproblematic concept is itself
a rather troubling one: as psychoanalysts know, behind what
appears to be innocuous and straightforward may lie the most
tortuous contradictions and lies. Narcissism is almost universally theorised as a defensive response to the inability to
construct a secure and stable self, this in turn being a result
of 'environmental deficiencies' – notably the inability of the
parents, themselves permeated by the infidelities of modernity,
to contain the infant's destructiveness or support her or his

demands for validation. But what if, in line with the arguments
of fashionable post-structuralists and postmodernists as well as
the doubts plaguing many who cannot remember what their
'self' was meant to be – what if this healthy self is a will-o'-the-
wisp? We pursue it and pursue it, we hunt and hunt, for there,
it seems, is the thing that will pull together all our disparate
sensations, experiences and desires. But what if it is unreal?
Who is the narcissist then?

It is Lacan who most cogently destabilises the possibility of
any notion of an integrated ego, and with it the broader but
more nebulous concept of the self. Like many psychoanalysts,
Lacan has an interest in mirrors; indeed, he names a
developmental phase in their honour. However, his mirror is
different from others. In, for example, Winnicott's influential
reading, the mother 'mirrors' the child's actual needs back to
the child, so that she or he can experience these needs as
tolerated and loved, and also can begin to symbolise them; the
more accurate and accepting the mirroring, the more space
there is for the true self to grow. This is a very beautiful image,
related to, but different from, the more intense descriptions of
containment derived from Kleinian theory. Someone watches
you and shows you they have understood what you are really
like, and that they accept it; this mirroring enables you to feel
appreciated and held and allows you to take more risks in
expressing your needs and making links with others. The lack
of distortion in the mirror enables an accurate subjective
rendering of the self.

Lacan, however, is not so poetic; he says more clearly than
anyone else that a mirror image is just an image and has no
real depth: 'the human being only sees his form materialised,
whole, the mirage of himself, outside of himself' (Lacan, 1975,
p. 140). The theory of the mirror phase is relevant here: the
idea that the ego is structured according to an external image
of the form of the individual effectively undermines notions of
mature or genuine or 'true' self that mirrors the world; we only
think it comes from inside. In addition, much that has gone
before is called into question by the Lacanian emphasis on the
speciousness of the mirroring process – the way what seems to
be an accurate message about the nature of the ego is in fact a
lie, pretending integrity when there is only a multiplicity of

incoherent drives and desires. One of the things that this suggests is that the notion of 'normal healthy relationships', endemic amongst theorists of narcissism, may be an ideological one, in the sense that it takes as given something which needs to be understood as constructed out of social processes. The 'normal, healthy' message given to the infant 'in the mirror' is that the ego has integrity and wholeness; but this message is a product of a particular mode of cultural organisation and perception, one which stresses the autonomy and psychological independence of individuals. So it is not just pathological forms of parenting and social organisation that produce people who are alienated from their real, true selves; *all* reflections of the self are false, for the self is a mirage. Is this a pessimistic doctrine? In many ways it is, as it removes the crutch of an appeal to human nature and basic needs in diagnoses of social pathology: if there is no such thing as a true self, a particular social order cannot be attacked for alienating people from it. On the other hand, the Lacanian doctrine does liberate us from the search for the 'truth' of human existence, or at least the truth of the self: if all organisations of the self are equally constructed, criteria for what is good have to be based on wider considerations than that of individualistic self-expression. In any event, given the distress and dissatisfaction attendant upon it, it seems unlikely that narcissism will be freed from its opprobrium even under Lacanian conditions of understanding.

Lacan (1975, p. 125) distinguishes, as does Freud, between two types of narcissism, which for him define the possibility of seeing and also experiencing a relationship.

First of all, there is, in fact, a narcissism connected with the corporeal image. This image . . . makes up the unity of the subject . . . In man . . . the reflection in the mirror indicates an original noetic possibility, and introduces a second narcissism. Its fundamental pattern is immediately the relation to the other . . . Narcissistic identification, . . . that of the second narcissism, is identification with the other which, under normal circumstances, enables man to locate precisely his imaginary and libidinal relation to the world in general.

The radical element in Lacan's argument here is his statement that, 'Narcissistic identification is identification with the other'. Because it is contextualised in the 'reflection in the mirror', this is not simply a statement concerning the significance of the identification process for development. Instead, it calls into question the distinction between self and other which is usually taken as the essential terrain of developmental history (individuation) and, indeed, of differentiations between sanity and madness. The reality of this self-other distinction, deemed fundamental by most psychoanalysts, philosophers and cultural critics (including Lasch), is denied in Lacan's statement, because it makes both unity of the subject and identification with the other into aspects of narcissism, both of them imaginary – the former a misreading of psychic unity as a parallel of bodily unity, the latter a phantasised experience of oneself as part of the world. Knowing the actual boundaries of one's self seems logically to be an essential prerequisite of true knowledge of the content of one's self – the kind of knowledge towards which psychoanalysis conventionally aspires. Lacan suggests that such knowledge is never substantive: a series of imaginary identifications lies behind the experience of the self as real, and as connected to others.

Discussing Freud's 'On Narcissism', Lacan throws down another challenge:

> Freud draws up a list of the different types of fixation in love, which has no reference whatsoever to what one might call a mature relationship – that myth of psychoanalysis. (1975, p. 132)

Not only narcissistic love, but 'anaclitic' love is also imaginary, 'since it is also based on a reversal of identification' (ibid.). Does this apply to all love? At least, the notion of an alternative, mature relationship is a myth. This does not mean that there are no differences in the quality of relationships, but it implies that the reality of a relationship is given not by its subjective impact, but by the structures surrounding it, by what (outside it) makes it possible and determines its shape. One more quotation makes this clear:

it's the symbolic relation which defines the position of the subject as seeing. It is speech, the symbolic relation, which determines the greater or lesser degree of perfection, of completeness, of approximation, of the imaginary. This representation allows us to draw the distinction between the *Idealich* and the *Ichideal*, between the ideal ego and the ego-ideal. The ego-ideal governs the interplay of relations on which all relations with others depend. And on this relation to others depends the more or less satisfying character of the imaginary structuration. (1975, p. 141)

According to Lacan, the ego ideal, originating from outside the subject, helps fix the nature of relationships; its reduction to the ideal ego, indeed to the notion of the self or 'ideal self' is a manifestation of how the symbolic can come to be captivated on the imaginary plane. That is, we see by means of our narcissism, we locate ourselves through dispersal of the ego in the world – we look all round for our image. And when we find it, we are satisfied, not realising that the way the world is really structured is hidden, for we are part of the structure and cannot see it all. Thus, the phantasy of a mature relationship which is not infiltrated by narcissism remains a phantasy: all relationships are constructed out of the interpellation of the ego (constructed from otherness, as the mirror phase theory makes clear) into the object. Moreover, the notion of a mature self or a mature relationship, while having relative value, cannot be a source of diagnostic certainty nor an image of social development.

Lacan's use of the concept of the ego ideal is very different from that of Chasseguet-Smirgel, described in the previous chapter; indeed, his reference to the 'ideal ego' is closer in tone to what she seems to have in mind. However, there is a significant point of convergence between these two French theories which are in other ways so different. Chasseguet-Smirgel, it will be recalled, contrasts the super-ego with the ego ideal, making it clear that she believes that it is only through the structural, three-person forms of the Oedipus complex that sufficient distance from absorption in the mother can be achieved. Following Grunberger, she argues that the narcissistic striving for unity characteristic of pre-Oedipal functioning is regressive because it is concerned with bringing about a return to a state of phantasised oneness with the other that denies difference, struggle and loss – that denies reality. Lacan's thought is different here, but it runs in part on some of the same lines. The Imaginary is summarised in the image of the mirror phase: there is a phantasised wholeness arising out of a presumed connection with the other, who in fact is a manifestation of unreality. It is the Symbolic which actually has more power – which fragments the phantasised narcissistic wholeness of the Imaginary by demonstrating how the possibility of a self-other relationship is actually fixed by something more powerful that stands outside it. This 'something', of course, is the father in the Oedipal triangle, or at least his word, his 'non' directed at the drive towards incestuous union; more broadly, it is the cultural and social Law.

Something outside the merger of self and other is needed if narcissism is to be surpassed – something paternal, in family terms. Interestingly, however, there are only rare mentions of fathers amongst the American and British theorists of narcissism; Kohut supplies one of them, but even that is limited to the idea that they may provide a 'second chance' for idealisation when the mother has failed to respond adequately to the infant's grandiosity. Otherwise, all is maternity: the security of the self, the modification of exhibitionism, the establishment of a realistic position in the world, these all derive from the mother's ability to support and contain her child's needs. It is in the maternal twosome that mental health or ill-health has its source; moreover, the perfect meeting of a subject's demand, the perfect union and relationship – the perfect primary narcissism – is a simple self-other absorption. But, in their different ways, Lacan, Grunberger and Chasseguet-Smirgel provide a reminder that there was such a being as Oedipus, that something always exists outside the self-other unit to say, 'you are a whole only in your head'. The full, healthy relationship is as imaginary as the manipulative one, if it is not located with some understanding of its symbolic significance, if it is not placed structurally. The easy designation of narcissistic pathology as distinct from mature object relationships is problematised by this claim, that there is no real relationship at all. And, finally, what about psychoanalytic theories which dwell so much on the mother-infant union that they have little or nothing to say about the father? Or, put more broadly, what about those who so fetishise the self and its 'true' maturation that they can see in the social world only an obstruction to healthy self-growth, rather than something that determines the structure of all development? In their avoidance of reality and escapist fantasies of wholeness and maturity, are not these theories narcissistic too?

Transference and change

Discussions of therapeutic interventions with narcissistic patients parallel the debates between Kleinian and object relational analysts on the relative worth of transference versus empathic modes. These debates reflect not just differences in technique, but also in outlook on what psychotherapy can offer – on the extent to which early deprivation can be made good by an accepting and maternal analyst (Frosh, 1987). In its final form, this represents a difference over the meaning of analytic 'cure'. Bromberg (1982) is pessimistic over the value of transference work with narcissistic patients, at least until late in the therapeutic relationship.

> The descendents of Narcissus now lie upon the analytic couch, as self-absorbed as ever, while behind them, as in the myth, sit the determined but still frustrated counterparts of Echo, trying to be heard. (pp. 444–5)

It is the mirroring function of the object for the narcissist that dominates the relationship with the analyst, swamping the transference and producing countertransference emotions centring on boredom, sleepiness and irritation. Bromberg describes the way the narcissist's grandiose self representation becomes fused to the '"need satisfying object" by a set of interpersonal operations designed to prevent the object from being little more than a mirror, and to keep the true nature of these operations "masked"' (p. 449). The analyst is seen neither as a 'real' person nor as a source of health-giving otherness for the patient, but as a reflection of the patient's own self, to be organised, manipulated and controlled – to be an echo and no more. But, as Kernberg notes, this echo is of something which is not really there.

> The narcissistic patient extends his own grandiosity to include the analyst and thus, while apparently free associating in the presence of the analyst, really talks to himself expanded into a grandiose 'self-observing' figure to which the patient becomes, temporarily, an attachment or satellite. (Kernberg, 1974, p. 258)

This attachment is different from psychotic merger because of its lack of real dependency and the way it is easily withdrawn at the end of the session, but there is a continuum, particularly where narcissistic pathology is part of a borderline personality structure – a counter-indication to psychoanalytic therapy, in Kernberg's view.

Kohut describes two types of narcissistic transference which he regards as 'pathognomic' for narcissistic personality disorders; predictably from his theory, they are the 'mirror transference', in which the unmet 'childhood need for a source of accepting-confirming "mirroring" is revived in the treatment situation' and the 'idealising transference' in which 'a need for merger with a source of "idealised" strength and calmness is similarly revived' (Kohut and Wolf, 1978, p. 176). Kohut (1971, p. 114) further distinguishes three forms of the mirror transference relating to different levels of pathology: (i) 'merger through the extension of the grandiose self', (ii) 'alter-ego transference or twinship' and (iii) 'mirror transference in the narrower sense'. These differ in the extent to which the analyst is experienced as a separate person rather than as a repository for, or reflection of, the patient's grandiose self, but even in the least primitive version (the 'mirror transference in the narrower sense') the transference relationship is superficial and unreal. At best, the analyst is experienced by the patient as a receptacle for the patient's own grandiose needs, tolerated only so long as she or he can sustain this position, offering admiration and support.

In the most mature and most developed form of the mirror transference the analyst is experienced as a separate person, but nonetheless one who becomes important to the patient and is accepted by him only to the degree that he is responsive to the narcissistic needs of the reactivated grandiose self. Thus, in the strictest sense of the mirror transference, the analyst's function becomes one of admiring and reflecting the grandiosity and exhibitionism of the patient. (Meissner, 1979, p. 417)

While the disintegration and oscillation of projections and introjections characteristic of borderline states may be avoided in narcissism, the unreality of their object relationships is fully reflected in the mirror of the transference; countertransferentially, boredom gives way to frustration and despair at the lack of impact of anything the analyst says or does, at the constant devaluation and meaninglessness of all interactions. This is a poignant concentration in the analytic space of the emptiness of many contemporary relationships.

Perhaps, additionally, this constitutes a finding out and exposure of an aspect of psychoanalysis' own pathology. The emptiness of contemporary culture presumably affects analysts as well as other people, so perhaps their willingness to put up with these tedious treatment relationships with boring patients is a kind of counterphobic behaviour, an attempt to master the emptiness through extensive contact with it, as one might master agoraphobia by becoming a long-distance lorry driver. Or perhaps, more straightforwardly, it is through the vicarious intensity of their probing relationships with their patients that analysts seek to overcome their own emptiness. Kernberg discusses the problems of unanalysed narcissism in psychoanalysts, but neglects a more general point, that the practice of psychoanalysis is one of the few ways in which intense relationships can be entered into without full commitment or accountability, with the defence of distance and professional control. How ironic it can be, then, when the analyst's counterphobic response to narcissistic fears of dependence is mimicked by the meaninglessness which the narcissistic patient brings into the consulting room. Controlling relationships from a safe distance? I will show you what real distance can be, and what it feels like to be controlled. Psychoanalytic practice as a defence against the boredom and superficiality of real life? I will bore you so you will think time will never move again.

Here perhaps Kernberg is correct in his criticisms of Kohut's therapeutic approach, although the situation is complex and it is dangerous to decide between opposing clinical positions on solely theoretical grounds. Kohut suggests that, 'since the central pathology in the narcissistic behaviour and personality disorders is the defective or weakened condition of the self, the goal of therapy is the rehabilitation of this structure' (Kohut and Wolf, 1978, p. 192). As he regards narcissistic pathology as essentially a reflection of a fixation at an early stage of self development, he proposes a therapeutic approach based on images of optimal mothering, particularly the empathic acceptance of the patient's grandiosity. As the mirror transference allows the 'transmuting internalisation' of an accepting and idealised selfobject, so the patient's pathological narcissism can have its sting removed, the self can be healed, and more mature forms of healthy narcissism adopted. Greenberg and Mitchell (1983) summarise:

> In analysis, the patient establishes a selfobject transference in either a mirroring or an idealising mode. This provides a kind of developmental second chance: the transmuting internalisation of the transferential relationship can become the core of a compensatory self structure. (p. 356)

Thus, Kohut reduces the significance of interpretations and instead emphasises the empathic acceptance of the patient's grandiosity, along with recognition of the analyst's failures of empathy (like the 'good enough' mother's) to help create the conditions under which the growth of the self can be resumed. The therapeutic efficacy of this approach cannot be judged here, although the difficulty of utilising traditional interpretive transference modes of work is well attested to throughout the analytic literature on narcissism and the congruence of some of Kohut's suggestions with Winnicott's notions of 'management' of schizoid patients is worth noting (see Frosh, 1987). But the underlying import of Kohut's procedure has some significant resonances. It is, explicitly, an advocacy of psychotherapy as 're-mothering', a process of making up to the patient for the inadequacies of her or his early parenting environment. It avoids challenge, hence avoiding the pent-up rage which Kohut as well as Kernberg detects behind the controlled mask of the narcissist. The analyst becomes the idealised object, the good rescuing figure who will create the first perfect and meaningful relationship in the narcissist's life, will provide compensation for the poor deal which she or he has had. This is an image of analysis which shares many attributes with the much-criticised notion of the 'corrective emotional experience'. It also seems to imply that psychoanalysis can replace reality, can create a new person by offering a better, more whole and accepting, early experience. Could this be wishful thinking, born out of the emptiness which narcissism so unremittingly reproduces? Or, perhaps, could the desire to be a totally good object for the patient be a reaction formation against the aggressive feelings which these patients provoke? Or a countertransferentially-driven reaction formation against the patient's own unconscious rage? What, in other words, does it suggest about what the analyst wants when she or he decides to accept the patient's grandiose yearnings and idealising tendencies?

Kernberg thinks Kohut's approach just leads to 'better adaptation of the grandiose self' without doing anything basic about it (1974, pp. 287–8). He argues that, because it is rage at early objects which is the central element in narcissistic pathology, transference work is crucial to effective analytic therapy. More precisely, as well as systematic interpretation of the positive transference, 'non-critical interpretation of the negative transference may help reduce the patient's fear of his own destructiveness and doubts about his goodness' (p. 268). Again, the issue of therapeutic efficacy cannot be judged here, although there is probably more likelihood of patients dropping out from Kernbergian than Kohutian therapy. But the image of what psychoanalysis can offer is significantly different in Kernberg's account, and perhaps superior in its recognition of the role and limitations of analytic work. Psychoanalysis analyses, and in the process seeks to enable people to encounter all their passions and to integrate their negativity into themselves. It does not try to replace, it does not construct a preferred, idealised reality, it cannot become a new process of parenting. It cannot change society, construct from a culture of narcissism a better culture of accepting and fully realised mature relationships. At its most hard-headed, in its Kleinian-inspired forms, psychoanalysis provides a setting which is tuned to allowing people to feel the full extent of their loss, the conventional and enforced failures of their early and formative world. Where Kohut implies an ability to be a better mother than the patient's actual mother, Kernberg offers only to allow the patient to understand and experience the full extent of her or his rage, without it blowing the world apart. This is an image of psychoanalysis neither as wish-fulfilment nor as acceptance, but as an enunciator of the full health of revolt against the imposed barrenness and empty glitter of a commodity-fetishising society.

Certainly this is an idealised view of Kernberg's non-idealising therapy. In practice, it is rarely possible to be sure what the forms and functions of psychoanalysis really are, what compromises are made, what rage avoided, what grandiosity mirrored and what superficiality reproduced. How should psychoanalysis itself escape the cultural imperatives which Lasch and Kovel so convincingly document, when, in Kovel's words, 'pathological narcissism is a pox of late capitalism' (1980, p. 199)? If all relationships are terrorised by the meaninglessness embedded in, and maintained by, contemporary social structures, then relationships between analysts and patients will also be terrorised in the same way, will be in danger of being rendered useless and void. In this context, it is an essential aspect of any full approach to narcissism to recognise its cultural determinants and imperatives. And, as a method of subversion, it is important to keep hold of the critical elements in psychoanalysis. These are: a refusal simply to mirror the surrounding world and its values; an avoidance of idealisation and escape; a willingness to recognise and validate rage and dissent; a constant process of challenge, of documenting the impact of social forces on individual psychological functioning.

Narcissism, perhaps because of the resonance it has for every individual in contemporary western society, is an area where real attempts have been made to produce a social understanding of pathology. Lasch (1979) notes that clinical studies can provide information for cultural understanding, and that is clearly true. But psychoanalysis needs the reciprocal process as well: to be properly and fully informed by an appreciation of how individual pathology links with, and is produced by, the pathologies of the social world. In the instance of narcissism, it seems that disturbance and normality begin to merge, something that always suggests the existence of a psychological state which is fixed in place by an external determinant, by the organisation of society. The disturbing nature of this society has been described in the modernist and postmodernist critiques. It is a society in which what is real slips away, merging with what is illusory, in which the image rules, in which people are immersed in dreams but dreams lose both their depth and their significance. Indeed, reality becomes dream-like in its constant, commodity-based promise of the fulfilment of desire; but this promise is eternally offered and removed, as the objects of desire are achieved and then found to be empty. Narcissism has its cultural roots in this tantalising cycle of excitement and deflation: the constant stream of apparently met, but actually frustrated desires leads to a denial both of the pain of genuine loss and of the struggle involved in achieving reparation, recognition and renewal. Narcissism as a commonly shared state of mind reflects, above all, the terrifying emptiness produced by the denial of reality.

Chapter 5

Dreaming of Madness

The habit of belief

In an archetypal postmodernist novel, Eco (1989) portrays the dangerous slippage between ecstatic fantasy and demonic reality. His protagonists construct a history of a Templar plot to control the world, a history in which they do not believe but in which they nevertheless invest enormous intellectual energy. Reflecting on the period of greatest excitement over this plot, the narrator notes,

> I believe that you can reach the point where there is no longer any difference between developing the habit of pretending to believe and developing the habit of believing . . . [All] of us were slowly losing that intellectual light that allows you always to tell the similar from the identical, the metaphorical from the real. We were losing that mysterious and bright and most beautiful ability to say that Signor A has grown bestial – without thinking for a moment that he now has fur and fangs. The sick man, however, thinking 'bestial,' immediately sees Signor A on all fours, barking or grunting. (pp. 467–8)

In the literature on psychosis, there is a series of troublesome Chinese boxes that reflect on this cultural confusion between what is image and what reality. First there is the general solipsism of the argument that as reality is always approached and activated through the perceptual process, then all perceptions are potentially equally valid: we cannot know the real, so any coherent fantasy will do – even if it receives no validation from the external world. 'Just because I'm paranoid, it doesn't mean that I'm not being persecuted,' is the

126

true, but nevertheless paranoid, version of this. Hopefully, this attack on the discriminatory powers of the intellect can be set aside: although our understanding can only approximate to reality through a series of perceptual guesses, reality can still be assumed to exist – outside our minds. The rose has thorns, even if all we know of it is its name.

The more mundane boxes, however, are more difficult to be rid of. At the level of therapeutic practice, too unmediated an exposure to the linguistic and perceptual confusion of psychotic experience, necessary for the therapeutic endeavour and for the completeness of psychoanalysis itself, may also threaten so to confuse the language and thought of the analyst that she or he will no longer be able to discriminate. The famous and terrifying countertransference in Lindner's (1954) 'jet propelled couch' is an example of this. Making no progress with a patient's presumably delusional belief that he lives as an alter-ego in an interplanetary world, the analyst decides to enter consciously into the fantasy himself. This has beneficial effects for the patient, but Lindner describes in a beautifully exact and self-reflective way how the consequence is that the fantasy almost takes him over instead.

> In the beginning it was a game. My wholesale acceptance of the fantasy was no more than a pretence, a device I had seized upon that promised to pry loose a disturbed mind from its adhesive clutch on a foundering life raft. But eventually it ceased to be a game, and the moves, the manœuvres, the manipulations of the pieces, passed from the hands of this player to become the tools of forces of which he was then hardly aware. (p. 281)

The analyst maintains the fantasy longer than does the patient – indeed, the patient keeps it going after he has ceased to believe in it so as not to disappoint the analyst, and it is only when he realises the shame of this that the analyst can himself become less deluded. A messy form of therapy, perhaps, but there might be an element of it in all interchanges between analysts and patients – one has to take the discourse of madness seriously, after all – and ensuring that the weirdness does not enter into the soul may be a difficult task.

The effects of this process on theory, too, should not be underestimated. Just as the individual analyst may start to share the delusional perceptions of the psychotic patient, so the theory developed to account for these perceptions may be so informed by psychotic speech that it too has delusional elements, thus reflecting rather than explaining the psychotic state of mind. Some of the theories to be encountered in this and the following chapter may turn out to contain elements of this kind. In addition, adoption of the allusiveness, word-play and inner-outer boundary loss characteristic of psychotic states occasionally seems to threaten the coherence of otherwise powerful accounts – a state of affairs that makes them both more poignant (because empathic) and more irritatingly hard to comprehend. Remembering how to maintain the boundaries of a metaphor, commenting on psychotic discourse without ennobling it, knowing the difference between signifier, signified and real: these are tasks of theory which are constantly under pressure when the object of that theory is the subversive theorisation implicit in psychotic thought.

The influencing machine

The psychotic experience, identified loosely with the clinical syndrome of schizophrenia, has, for some cultural commentators, become emblematic of the postmodern state of mind. This usage comes partly from a sense that the schizophrenic experience is in some way *normal* in the modern world, expressing the actual state of existence of ordinary people, notable only because of its extreme clarity of manifestation. So the widespread contemporary difficulty people have in establishing an integrated selfhood, the apparent breakdown of rationality and personal autonomy, the suspicion that each of us is really under the control of someone or something else, the explosion of unmasterable masses of computer-generated information – all these modern sensations are reminiscent of what is thought to be the psychotic state of fragmentation and personal dissolution. Sliding the signified under the signifier, losing the substance beneath the image and the image of the image: if I no longer own myself (if I never did), who owns me?

To some extent, psychoanalysis' notion of the unconscious reflects this sensation of out-of-controlness, of not knowing what is the truth of our selves. 'There is no stronger evidence that we have been successful in our effort to uncover the unconscious,' claims Freud, 'than when the patient reacts to it with the words "I didn't think that", or "I didn't (ever) think of that"' (1925, p. 442). The more strong the negation, the more important the truth of what has been negated. In psychoanalytic thought, this is not simple deceptiveness, or even 'bad faith'; it is a radical alienation of the symbolised and rational self from the real sources of intention and desire. 'I didn't think that, it thought me.' Something speaks through each one of us, something of which we are unconscious; this is taken to be a general truth about human nature. Thus, there can be no settled normality of the self, only a series of provisional organisations through which the underlying discourses of the unconscious make themselves felt. As Freud notes, these discourses are of a particularly discordant and uncontrollable kind:

> exemption from mutual contradiction, primary process (mobility of cathexes), timelessness, and replacement of external by psychical reality – these are the characteristics which we may expect to find in processes belonging to the system UCs. (Freud, 1915, p. 191)

In the unconscious there are all sorts of different ideas, memories and desires from different periods, with characteristics which differ radically from one another and are sometimes opposed, abiding side-by-side as if nothing made any difference, as if there were no shades of time or tensions of contradiction – no right or wrong, before or after, surface or depth. Read like this, the unconscious is a truly postmodern arena, a cacophony of jangling dissonances experienced as the true and normal human state. To the extent that this is the case, there is no need to look further for a psychoanalysis of the postmodern mind.

The ordinary relations between conscious and unconscious, however, are not unfettered enough to catch the full flavour of the postmodernist free fall. Indeed, as described in Chapter 2, the Freudian imagery of thrusting drive held back by desperate defence in the service of the preservation of civilisation, works more persuasively as a *modernist* metaphor for the revolutionary upsurge constantly threatening to overturn the established order. This has an 'order threatened by chaos' structure, characteristic of modernist imagery; moreover, the experiential norm is given in psychoanalysis as one in which the individual feels in control, with unconscious desires sufficiently sublimated to allow for their moderate satisfaction without the destruction of the necessities of social life. In other words, traditional psychoanalysis sides in the end with order, with a mode of rationality that recognises the existence and the rights of unconscious desire, but strives to restrict its expression to clearly bounded and usually socially validated channels.

In the postmodern world, by contrast, the dominant experience is said to be that of the impossibility of maintaining such a balance between desire and reality without the sacrifice of selfhood. This is closer to psychosis than to normality, or even neurosis, in which the sensation of a real and central self is sustained, however troubled it may be. Psychosis appears with the loss of such a central self, accompanied by bombardment by psychological processes operating in a raw form, with nothing to integrate them – projective identification with a barely existent ego, for example. It is, to paraphrase Lacan, to be spoken rather than speaking. Thus, 'the subject in the postmodern age is often dubbed "psychotic" because there is "no centre" around which to unite or "resolve the various voices" that speak the postmodern citizen' (Finlay, 1989, p. 46). The norm of displacement, disaffection and disorientation by which contemporary society is characterised is, in this reading, not merely the breeding-ground for narcissism, but the summary form of psychotic fragmentation.

Tausk's (1933) pre-postmodernist description of the schizophrenic 'influencing machine' presents in a kind of silent-movie form the precise sense of mystery, disintegration and persecution which has dominated so much of modern western culture.

This influencing machine, complained of by some schizophrenics,

> is a machine of a mystical nature. The patients are able to give only vague hints of its construction. It consists of boxes, cranks, levers, wheels, buttons, wires, batteries and the like . . . All the discoveries of mankind, however, are regarded as inadequate to explain the marvellous powers of this machine, by which the patients feel themselves persecuted. (p. 50)

Persecution, particularly in the form of thought-insertion and withdrawal, is the function of the machine: 'Its construction cannot be explained, but its function consists in the transmission or "draining off" of thoughts and feelings by one or several persecutors' (ibid.). In addition, the victim of the machine experiences sexually enervating bodily feelings and a technological mass of inexplicable but clearly modern invasive powers.

> It creates sensations that in part cannot be described, because they are strange to the patient himself, and that in part are sensed as electrical, magnetic, or due to air currents. (p. 50)

Although Tausk views the machine as a consequence of already-existing persecutory ideas, the main impact of his description is to convey the way the schizophrenic patient experiences inner change as originating in a mysterious external form which is nevertheless intensely material and machinic. It is like a deranged version of a Futurist cartoon: an extrinsic mechanical device of no knowable construction, mystifying but immensely powerful, able to enter into one's mind, take over one's thoughts, bring about transformations which are alienating 'estrangements' of the self. The machine as a whole cannot be comprehended; even when the victim seems to understand its construction, 'it is obvious that this feeling is, at best, analogous to that of a dreamer who has a feeling of understanding, but has not the understanding itself' (p. 55).

It is easy to see why Tausk's paper has become a classic psychoanalytic exploration of the phenomenology of psychosis. It is also easy to appreciate its attractiveness for enthusiastic unmaskers of contemporary pathology. The portrait of the influencing machine is not just a recognition of the impact of the machine age on the modern imagination; it is also a precognition of the deeply unsettling power of information machines – computers in all their myriad forms – to summarise, persuade, digest and 'influence' us in such a way that we no longer feel in control. The influencing machine is a persecutory advertiser, or perhaps it is the other way round: the advertiser as a subtle and seductive persecutory machine. Paranoia is the normal state of affairs in the postmodern world, a paranoia well founded on the activities of eaves-droppers, information-manipulators, liars. Nothing and no-one can be trusted: they may know us better than we know ourselves, and will always put this knowledge to their own use. Influencing machines are all around, we are part of some global network which is incomprehensible to us all; we think we know it, but the meaning slips away, as in our dreams and nightmares. From this perspective, it is paranoia which is the element in psychosis that is emblematic of contemporary society: not so much fragmentation as technological persecution.

Tausk's vision, however, already seems dated. The paranoid form of schizophrenic phantasy, which does indeed often seem to be the state of modern social relations, is not by itself a sufficiently accurate metaphor for the fragmentation and disintegration stressed by postmodernists; on the contrary, in fact, paranoid delusions are generally very well organised and even persuasive. To that extent, they emanate from a distorted rather than a disintegrated self: they are often a mechanism of defence against that final dissolution. Contrastingly, it is the loss of ego-other boundaries, the dispersal of the self rather than its preservation as a cherished but victimised object, which is the focus of interest for the postmodern colonists of the imagery of psychosis. What they take to be the characteristic contemporary experience is not the threat of the influencing machine as something impinging on the individual from outside, but as something which has already entered – and destroyed – the soul. The kind of psychosis with which they are concerned, therefore, is the kind in which the self has been broken into bits.

There are several difficulties with this. For example, if psychotic fragmentation is so pervasive, how is the ordinary interaction of individuals (no selves to call their own), sustained? If we are all narcissists, it is imaginable: we just use others as mirrors of ourselves, empty vessels threatened by envy and rage. But what kind of social intercourse is possible if we are all mad? Either it is a collective delusion (everyone believes the same weird thing, so all get along fine together) or our intercourse with others takes the form of interpenetration – one mental space merging with another, with all the sexuality of the imagery drained away. In neither case is it obvious how relationships can begin and grow or commitments form and deepen. In a similar way, using psychosis as a metaphor for normal postmodern functioning produces a pessimistic reading of the possibilities for resistance. If all our selves are so dispersed by the penetrative power of the dislocations of modernity, then what can be done to oppose this force, to imagine or construct some alternative way of being? The pessimism of a theory is not necessarily an indication of its falsity, but there is something tautological – or, perhaps, of the nature of an infinite regress – about a theory that proposes both that every individual is broken apart by paranoid dread, and that the social world is in its essence persecutory. If we can perceive accurately that the world is persecutory, then we are not paranoid (or not completely paranoid); indeed, inculcation of a view suggesting that all our perceptions are psychotic delusions may be a way of strengthening those persecutory tendencies which actually do exist. Intolerance of doubt is a rigid defence employed to stave off psychotic dissolution, but total doubt of absolutely every aspect of one's experience is that dissolution itself.

But this really is too infinitely regressive. The psychotic process is clearly one which has resonance for postmodernists, as indeed it has resonated at many points in history. The mad are not only always with us, they clearly always have had something important to say. Foucault (1967) has influentially reproduced this voice; Bernauer (1987) provides a summary specially designed to link with postmodern ideas. For Foucault, he says,

> Madness is that constantly changing region of human experience which defies any regulating intentionality; which speaks in the language of the fantastic and the passionate; which dwells not merely in historical time but also in a violent, timeless stream of subversion, flooding the secure banks of what is positively known about the order of the self and the world. (p. 348)

This reading of Foucault makes his a celebration of the otherness of madness, its continuing reminder of the existence of an order of things which is opposed to the rationality so characteristic of modernity (the isometry of images of madness with those of femininity is no accident here). Bernauer goes further here, perhaps further than Foucault himself.

> The plight of the psychotic's loss of self serves as a warning of what might occur to one who no longer follows modernity's path of self-development and self-knowledge, that task of binding ourselves to a positive nature that a specific teleology of the self has fabricated and on which it has conferred a truth status . . . Psychosis represents a rupturing of bonds with modern identity, but in such a way as to be confined in a place of silent exteriority to our culture. (p. 357)

This leaves open at least two possibilities. first, psychosis could be seen as a particularly sensitive response to the real conditions of our time. Psychotic experiences are not absolutely the same as those of normal postmodern subjects; they are dissociated, entrapped, deeply painful and disturbing. But they bear a connection with a social order which indeed is also like that: embodied in these particularly susceptible individual schizophrenics is a reflection of the deepest pathologies of our time. Levin (1987), for instance, takes schizophrenia to be a commentary on what he calls the 'nihilism' of contemporary culture, its construction of the self as split off from others and, alongside this, of the mind as divorced from the body. Schizophrenic symptoms express this cultural split between inner and outer, public and private; the psychotic confusion between what is self and what other, what mental and what material, expresses the poignant suffering which accompanies the entire western project of selfhood.

> The inner-outer split and the Self-Other split encourage paranoia; but since they also encourage intolerance, bigotry, hatred, conflict and aggression, paranoid fantasies of panoptical and acoustic surveillance, thought control and attacks of demonic possession should not be immediately dismissed as symptoms of private madness: it could be argued that they manifest an awareness that may be in touch with a normally concealed reality, a normally concealed sociopathy, the social genesis of a form of suffering represented only in its most extreme state by the classified schizophrenic. (p. 526)

This acknowledges the suffering involved in schizophrenic breakdown, but places the psychotic process on a continuum with ordinary reality: in particularly attuned or predisposed people, the pathological underpinnings of nihilistic western culture are expressed in the form of breakdown. Schizophrenic sufferers, therefore, are disturbed, but what disturbs them is the underlying disturbance of modernity.

For Glass (1987), writing in the same collection as Levin, schizophrenia is even more closely attuned to the political realities of contemporary society.

> The language and logic of delusion constitute a commentary on power; schizophrenic narrative abounds with messages about victimisation, domination, enslavement, grandiosity . . . For the schizophrenic . . . what delusion 'speaks' provides a frame of reference, and within its knowledge systems (or logics) lie symbolic messages directed at relations that describe political life: power, authority, rights, domination, justice and injustice. (p. 406)

What schizophrenia reveals by its parody of politics, is how
mad political life is – how divorced from its own emotional
roots, how deeply founded on the repression of real needs, how
completely caught up and distorted it is by the acting out of
phantasies of power.

> What is called 'pathological' in the setting of the mental
> hospital becomes 'normal' and sane under the power of the
> rational consensus in defining political acts as good or bad,
> justifiable or unjustifiable. (Glass, 1987, p. 416)

Thus, psychosis acts out something deeper in western culture;
when embodied in the schizophrenic individual, it is an
internalisation of a pathology which is widespread. This is a
generally acceptable notion in some ways, registered in the
discussions on narcissism in the previous two chapters. But the
exactness of the analogy is open to question; the reading of
psychosis may recognise the suffering it produces, but its
detailing of the phenomenology of the psychological processes
involved is so general as to make it possible to see psychosis as
emblematic of almost any form of social oppression. Levin sees
the inner/outer confusions of the psychotic as expressive of the
denial of the interconnectedness of selves characteristic of
modernity (or only of capitalism?). Glass sees them as part of
a wide critique of the distortions of political structure and
process. As portrayals of social ills, these are suggestive and
even penetrating accounts. But what is *psychotic* about psychosis, what is the particular nature of this psychological
configuration and how does it connect with the actual
workings of the social world? Not just as metaphor, but as a
specific product of social and interpersonal forces?
     The 'psychosis as expressive of social ills' position has much
to recommend it, but requires a more detailed analysis of the
psychological processes embedded in psychotic breakdown
than the paralleling exercises described so far can achieve.
But before considering this further, there is a second possible
reading of psychosis available from the post-Foucaultian
perspective. This is that psychosis could be a strategy of
opposition, not necessarily consciously chosen, in which the
constraints of modernity are liquidated by the impassioned

resistance of the 'timeless stream of subversion' manifested in the psychotic individual. The extreme nature of the psychotic experience is a measure of the extremity of modern repression; Bernauer (1987) suggests that 'one of the specifically modern features of psychosis' may be its embeddedness in a social world in which power has become fundamentally repressive, making resistance 'an issue of either-or, total Refusal or total Submission' (p. 358). Psychosis is that 'total Refusal', an heroic act of repudiation of contemporary oppression that results in a complete estrangement from reality as the rest of us know it. Psychosis, therefore, is not the mode of functioning of all under the conditions of modernity; rather, it is what happens to those who have seen the modern world for what it is, and said no.

Schizoanalysis

The most influential modern romanticist of madness was probably Laing, whose strikingly original establishment of the intelligibility of psychotic communications in *The Divided Self* (1959) was one of the most important starting points for the antipsychiatry movement. As discussed elsewhere (Banton *et al*, 1985), the trajectory of Laing's work in the 1960s was towards a gradual broadening of the context employed to make schizophrenia comprehensible – from the existential state of the individual, to her family context, to, in *The Politics of Experience* (1967), the whole mad world. As we noted, in this book Laing made 'a leap from insanity as an *intelligible* response, to madness as a *rational* response to circumstances. Madness becomes sanity' (Banton *et al*, 1985, p. 69). The problems with this work are legion: an undervaluing of the distress and suffering involved in the schizophrenic state of mind, a crude view of society as a homogeneously oppressive mass, a straightforwardly oppositional presentation of the individual (good) versus society (bad) that drifts into an essentialist rendering of the nature of the self. All this has been documented well in some commentaries which cannot be rejected as simple ideological statements of the pro-psychiatry position (e.g. Sedgwick, 1982; Hirst and Woolley, 1982). But there are also some dazzling insights in Laing's early work (particularly *The Divided Self*) which are worth remembering as we move into a consideration of a more fashionable presentation of the 'madness as rebellion' point of view.

First, Laing's work was rooted in a genuine attempt to understand the detail of psychotic breakdown from the 'inside': for example, no-one has ever presented a more powerful, evocative or poignantly persuasive 'case history' than Laing, in the 'Ghost of the Weed Garden' section of *The Divided Self*. Indeed, it is as he moves further away from such detailed study that his writing becomes both vaguer and less convincing: *The Politics of Experience* is good on poetic evocation, weak on politics, weaker still on analysis of individual 'experience'. Secondly, Laing's utilisation of the interior point of view – of the empathic phenomenological method – in his account of psychosis makes it intelligible in a very specific context, that of warped, degraded or disturbed childhood relationships. This is, of course, a psychoanalytic perspective, although Laing's use of existential theory and phenomenological method tends to divert attention away from this element of his thought. But what is going on here is important: Laing is at his most persuasive when he is closest to his material, whether it is the 'word salad' of the individual schizophrenic patient or the multiple dialogues of family life. At these points, the psychotic experience and the psychological processes lying behind it come to life: they are seen as a disintegration of ego-other boundaries, a loss of personal boundedness ('ontological insecurity'), and a pervasive mystification of self- and inter-personal communications. Once he moves away from these details, generalises to all of society, the focus goes: schizophrenia is evoked as 'hypersanity', one of the few credible modes of transcendence of the madness of the world, but the feel of the psychotic state of mind disappears. By being used merely for oppositional purposes, psychosis becomes little more than a slogan. The message from this seems to be that if psychosis is to be used as a portrait of the depravity of contemporary society, it must be painted with very specific and detailed brush strokes.

The great postmodern psychoanalytic and anti-psychoanalytic text is *Anti-Oedipus* (Deleuze and Guattari, 1972). It is 'anti-psychoanalytic' because it opposes traditional and Lacanian theory and practice, particularly excoriating the Oedipal structure which is seen as the imposition of a controlling and disempowering lattice on the free flows of desire. But it is also psychoanalytic, because it embraces the unconscious, because it is within the terms of a Lacanian-inspired psychoanalysis that all its discourse is framed, even though it is also 'anti-Lacanian' in its opposition to Lacan's theory of desire as arising out of lack. Schizoanalysis, the practice which derives from the political and psychological work in *Anti-Oedipus*, is described by Deleuze and Guattari explicitly as a form of psychoanalysis, 'a political and social psychoanalysis, a militant analysis' (p. 98). Thus it is psychoanalytic and anti-psychoanalytic at one and the same time, a total critique and revision of psychoanalysis, proposed in terms of the unconscious. And *Anti-Oedipus* is also postmodern because of its interest in dismantling grand theory and unifying structure, conventional forms of order and control, in favour of a celebration of multiplicity and revolution, specific points of contact with desire. Schizoanalysis is concerned with finding a way out from the entrapping webs of Oedipal and capitalist discourse, into a mode of being that valorises positivity over lack, molecular over molar, fragments and partial objects over wholes, schizophrenia over neurosis. Hence Foucault's prefatory celebration of Deleuze and Guattari's celebration of the fragments: he summarises the principles of living to be garnered from *Anti-Oedipus* as,

> withdraw allegiance from the old categories of the negative (law, limit, castration, lack, lacuna), which Western thought has so long held sacred as a form of power and an access to reality. Prefer what is positive and multiple, difference over uniformity, flows over unities, mobile arrangements over systems. Believe that what is productive is not sedentary but nomadic. (Foucault, 1972, p. xiii)

In the terms of this postmodernist analysis, nothing represents anything else, there are no symbols or hidden meanings; all that is just is. Everything apparently integrative is fake, an attempt to quiet the jubilant anarchism of desire; the truth lies in immediate impressions, elementary signifiers; the unconscious cannot be organised, it is a loose confederation of desire-producing machines, 'desiring-machines', concrete bits and beings. Schizoanalysis does not look for hidden meanings in this, for representations or underlying, interpretable signifieds; it savours the play of signifiers, the juxtaposition of one free sound or inscription against another. Such are the postmodernist terms of contemporary experience: one bit of information thrown against another; they meet and part, in their trajectories lies all their significance, there is nothing else.

There is an intrinsic link, write Deleuze and Guattari, between capitalism and schizophrenia. This is not just, as most interpretations (including Laing's) have it, because capitalist society drives people mad, but because the production of schizophrenia is part and parcel of capitalist production: 'our society produces schizos the same way it produces Prell shampoo or Ford cars, the only difference being that the schizos are not saleable' (p. 245). Capitalism, like schizophrenia, systematically removes traditional and socially pre-ordained limitations, outmoded restrictions and pre-given barriers; in the language of schizoanalysis it 'deterritorialises' – removes desire from territorial restraint – by freeing the productive processes in the interests of pure production. Capitalism puts production first: anything which stands in the way of this is swept aside. Thus, the end point of capitalism, claim Deleuze and Guattari, is the dismantling of all meaning, the production of consumption without end; in this way the capitalist process mimics the schizophrenic process. In schizophrenia, too, there is no limit, no restriction of meaning, no 'territorialisation'; there is only desire driving forward endlessly. 'When we say that schizophrenia is our characteristic malady, the malady of our era, we do not merely mean to say that modern life drives people mad. It is not a question of a way of life, but a process of production' (p. 34). For desire and production are at one in the case of schizophrenia, which is as they should be:

> desire is a machine, a synthesis of machines, a machinic arrangement – desiring machines. The order of desire is the order of *production*; all production is at once desiring-production and social production. We therefore reproach

psychoanalysis for having stifled this order of production, for having shunted it into *representation*. (p. 296)

However, Deleuze and Guattari are not wholly enamoured with capitalism, as may seem from this. For them, the capitalist process only looks like the schizophrenic one because of its tendency to sweep away pre-existing boundaries. But it has not the same absolute freedom and celebratory flow and flux as schizophrenia, because it still obeys an overarching set of principles, those of capital and profit. Capitalism's *relative* deterritorialisation is, therefore, not a full deterritorialisation, because it substitutes for pre-capitalist codes 'an extremely rigorous axiomatic that maintains the energy of the flows in a bound state on the body of capital as a socius that is deterritorialised, but also as a socius that is even more pitiless than any other' (p. 246). Capitalism presents itself as freedom (the 'free market', for instance), but is in fact an immensely effective system of ultimate oppression, allowing no way out from its own terms of existence. Schizophrenia, on the other hand, is the complete dismantling of codes, the 'absolute limit' of all societies that 'causes the flows to travel in a free state on a desocialised body without organs' (ibid.). Thinking about the production of a revolutionary subject, Deleuze and Guattari write that, 'a schizophrenic out for a walk is a better model than a neurotic lying on the analyst's couch' (p. 2). And this schizophrenic 'nomad' is a hero:

> The schizophrenic deliberately seeks out the very limit of capitalism: he is its inherent tendency brought to fulfilment, its surplus product, its proletariat and its exterminating angel. He scrambles all the codes and is the transmitter of the decoded flows of desire . . . Schizophrenia is desiring-production at the limit of social production. (p. 35)

So modern society appears to free, but in fact places people under the sway of a generalised control; the complete break-down/breakthrough comes only with the schizophrenic process. Not with the schizophrenic *sufferer*, however: Deleuze and Guattari do not quite slip into creating a romance out of the ordinary psychotic patient. Instead, they differentiate between process – the activation of the psychotic deconstruction of imposed reality – and concrete schizophrenic sufferers, who in fact are suffering from the failure of the process to become complete. These sufferers have had their schizophrenic process restricted and interrupted – they become Oedipalised or catatonic or perverse. Indeed, Deleuze and Guattari see no opposition between neurosis and psychosis: the former is produced by the latter, or rather by the particular way in which the schizophrenic process is thwarted. 'What makes the schizophrenic ill . . . What transforms the breakthrough into a breakdown?' ask Deleuze and Guattari of themselves. 'It is the constrained arrest of the process, or its continuation in the void, or the way it is forced to take itself as a goal' (p. 362). The full process is not the chronic schizophrenic patient long forgotten on the long-stay ward; it is, rather, a process of escape and liberation, the breakdown of meaning, representation, order, imposition, control. It is the full play of desiring machines, of partial objects; it is the opposition to capitalism through the final breakdown of all territorialisation. Schizoanalysis contributes to this by opposing the ordering of desire into meaningful and controllable blocks and by working towards the disintegration of the normal ego.

> The task of schizoanalysis is that of tirelessly taking apart egos in their presuppositions; liberating the pre-personal singularities they enclose and repress; mobilising the flows they would be capable of transmitting, receiving or intercepting; establishing always further and more sharply the schizzes and breaks well below conditions of identity; and assembling the desiring-machines that countersect everyone and group everyone with others. (p. 362)

Everything flows, everything is in motion, rushing through, production without end.

This schizoanalysis, deconstructive, non-respecting of ego and identity, immersed in fluidity – this claims to be the truly postmodern psychoanalysis, celebrating breakdown and psychotic fragmentation, understanding it as the breaking through of the full and eloquent forces of unconscious desire. Where Lacanian psychoanalysis understands desire as a product of lack, as an impossible gesture towards the achievement of what has been radically split off from the subject, schizoanalysis emphasises the positive nature of desire – its expressiveness, aliveness, refusal of control or of limitation. Desire is to be celebrated and the ultimate celebration is to be found in the activity of disconnection, eruption, breaking out. Such desire is not representational, it does not express something else: it is what it is, its meaning inherent in its productivity. Schizoanalysis glorifies breakdown of the self in aid of, as part of, the breakthrough process; it validates the snapping of the signifying chain, the free play of signifiers, each invested with their own elemental charge. Such is, indeed, a schizophrenic process.

Deleuze and Guattari claim the creation of the revolutionary subject, whose name is schizophrenia; the schizophrenic process is seen as the end point of modernity, its total deconstruction. Holding this in mind, schizoanalysis is dedicated towards the encouragement of this process, for with it comes revolutionary transformation – a revolutionary psychoanalysis. All the excitement of anarchism, or maybe of nihilism, can be found in this remarkable book. And yet, something seems odd here. Perhaps it is the way in which the revolutionary alternative seems to bear a disturbing similarity to the currently existing postmodern condition, at least as described by postmodernists. There, too, can be found the celebration of fragmentation, of signifiers without signifieds, shards of experience without any representational function. There, too, is the opposition to psychoanalysis' concern with interpretive significance on the grounds that it is a seductive but false, ideologically-driven attempt to place narrative coherence above the truth of unorganisable particles of meaning. Play, switching between channels of being, juxtaposition rather than integration, breaking out of bounds – this is the celebratory element in the postmodern condition. But disturbance is there, too: the sense of rootlessness and emptiness, while liberating people from traditional constraints, also makes them homeless. It removes succour and connection, it atomises. Moreover, it removes, without replacement, the traditional defence offered to people by humanism: the sense that there is something meaningful within, some selfhood which cannot be voluntarily renounced nor involuntarily exploited or taken away by others. That is, what is presented in *Anti-Oedipus* as glorious freedom, is actually, to the extent that it can be glimpsed in current reality, neither glorious nor free at all.

Deleuze and Guattari's portrait of psychosis is also problematic. Is it reasonable to celebrate it as the best way out of capitalism? Kovel, who has dedicated much of his career to preserving the radical elements in psychoanalysis, comments as follows on the vision of schizophrenia in *Anti-Oedipus*.

> Unhappily, the ontology with which its arguments are laboriously advanced is so twisted out of shape that it itself qualifies for delusional status. For in order to prime the 'schizo' for his emancipatory role, the authors somehow neglect to put schizophrenia in a real light, denying the terror of annihilation and the autism that ensues upon the break . . . Yes, there is an amazing uncodable flow to the schizophrenic's inner world – but it occurs at the price of desociation, and all the 'schizoanalysis' in the world won't put Humpty Dumpty together again. (1987, p. 343)

Kovel, in drawing his own picture of schizophrenia, opposes most of the elements in the one produced by Deleuze and Guattari. Or, rather, his valuation of the nature of the schizophrenic experience and of the psychotic process is opposite to that of the schizoanalysts – it has a consistently negative sign compared to the positivity which they emphasise. So Kovel recognises the 'radical estrangement' of the psychotic from normal experience, but this is not because of some breakthrough of a new and bolder consciousness; instead, it is regarded as a mode of non-being, of total alienation from self as well as other. 'The centre of schizophrenia,' writes Kovel, 'is annihilation: the person becoming schizophrenic remains materially present and conscious, but ceases to be' (p. 336). This state is not, *pace Anti-Oedipus*, one of liberatory freedom or creative emancipation, but one of overwhelming destructiveness coupled with a desperate attempt to retain some semblance of subjectivity. Thus, using ideas closely related to the material on projective identification to be discussed in the next chapter, Kovel describes how the schizophrenic, her or his subjectivity slipping away into a void of non-being, tries to restore the shattered threads of the self by taking in bits and pieces of the world – however malignant they may be. Rather than rejoicing in escape from oppressive structures, the schizophrenic process is characterised, in this view, by despairing efforts to recover what has been lost. Hallucinations and delusions are not some better way of being, some new vision, however poetic they may seem at times; they are attempts to people an inner world which has lost all its content. Hence, there is a radical and irredeemable gap between the schizophrenic and the creative individual – the truly utopian revolutionary, for example. Where the artist can switch in and out of her or his vision, the schizophrenic has lost both subjectivity and intersubjectivity; the schizophrenic is surely spoken rather than speaking, but this pure operation of desire, as Deleuze and Guattari might view it, signifies only that the sufferer cannot say what she or he wants. This is, once again, no model for radical protest.

> The schizophrenic reveals not emancipation but the negative of emancipation: not unfree but antifree. The critical negativity within being – the capacity to refuse the given world while remaining one's self – is demolished and transposed to the zone of nonbeing, where self as well as world are refused, broken down, then commingled into the autistic configuration. (Kovel, 1987, p. 343)

Deleuze and Guattari would probably counter that this confuses the schizophrenic patient with the schizophrenic process, but whether the one can be envisaged without the other seems questionable. The abstraction of 'process' is little more than nihilism unless it is pinned to the concreteness of experience; once that occurs, one is in the realm of psychology and hence of real people. More strongly, what Kovel's argument implies is that the schizophrenic process is distinct from the revolutionary one: the latter entails the preservation of self while the world is changed, the former involves the dissolution of self and world together. Schizophrenia is not, in this reading, the revolutionary opposite to capitalism, it is just something capitalism produces or makes worse. So, Kovel presents a humanistic reading: the conditions for the construction of selfhood are always fragile; modernity makes them more so, with its focus on production and consumption, and its relegation of human subjects to the status of interchangeable objects. Capitalism and schizophrenia are not opposites; they go hand in hand.

> For all its wealth and power, capitalist society turns out to be one of the worst settings possible in which to be schizophrenic . . . Fragmentary and chaotic family experience, intrusion by the administered consciousness of the mass media, lack of an organic community – all these features of late capitalist life contribute to a weakened sense of self and to the dissolution of intersubjective relations. (pp. 341–2)

The same conditions, that is, that produce narcissism are linked with psychosis: the undermining of self in the former reaches its absolute in the latter

The madness of self and society

The various energetic attempts to employ psychosis as an emblem of the disturbance of contemporary society seem to have produced as much contradiction as they have light. For some, schizophrenia is the normal state of affairs produced by modernity, which is a fragmenting experience leaving all of us with no core of self nor stable essence. The psychotic's perception of the world is of a whirling confusion, voices inside and outside the head, persecutory forces waiting to pounce, nothing making sense. Under modern conditions, this is rather an accurate portrayal of what the world is really like. So the dominant psychological experience of all people is that of psychosis: the messages surrounding us really are meaningful only in a persecutory sense, as capitalism grinds into its final gear. Everyone struggles to find their own place to stand in this maelstrom, their own imaginary self to stave off the deconstructing forces all around. Those that succeed relatively well stay 'sane', but their deeper experiences are still those of the madness which is acted out in the more concrete and obvious symptomatology of schizophrenics. Moreover, their very sanity is a kind of imaginary position, a specious covering over of the dissolution produced by the unintegrateable social forces out of which our selves are constructed.

For other theorists, schizophrenic breakdown is what happens to people who are particularly attuned to the dramas and disturbances of modernity. 'Normal' life exists and is not the same as psychosis, but behind it lies a deeply pathogenic social structure. What psychosis represents is a kind of return of the repressed of modern society – a bursting out of the hidden emotions and traumas produced by systematic violations of humanity and sanity. The ideology of rationality, for example, covers up a darkly irrational structure of politics and social relations, an irrationality reflected, as Laing noted, in the technologically brilliant violence and destructiveness of the twentieth century. Psychotic breakdown is, in true psychoanalytic fashion, to be interpreted both as symptomatic and expressive of this disturbance: symptomatic in that it indicates the existence of pathology, expressive in that it acts out in symbolic form what the nature of the disturbance might be. So the dissolution of selfhood, the confusion of inner-outer boundaries, the persecutory phantasies, the whole 'influencing machine' network of sensations characteristic of various forms of schizophrenia – all these say first that there is a conflict between human needs and what the social order can offer, and, secondly, that this conflict centres on the necessary conditions for the establishment of a secure and stable self. Even more than is the case for narcissists, in this reading, psychotics express the deep denial of emotion and nurture which is characteristic of the buzzing persecutory confusion of the modern environment. Indeed, the distinction between the psychotic and the narcissist may actually be that the former correctly observes and focuses on the persecutory element in modernity, while the narcissist knows only that her or his needs are not being met. That is, the distinction between narcissism and psychosis is not just one of severity; it is also clarity of vision. The narcissist survives because she or he manages to maintain a sufficiently coherent blind spot to believe that it is possible to preserve some vestige of selfhood in the face of the failure of the parents to offer a real experience of care. The psychotic, on the other hand, sees only too well that at the heart of modernity is a vicious attack on its subjects.

The visionary status of the schizophrenic is also what is emphasised by the third position described in this chapter – the schizophrenic as revolutionary or, in the version adopted by the authors of *Anti-Oedipus*, the psychotic process as the antagonist to capitalism. Thus, the psychotic is the Great Refuser, the one who will not go along with the constraints and distortions of the dominant social order. Psychosis breaks down barriers, 'deterritorialises', sets free drives, passions and desires, hears voices which are normally denied, sees visions usually hidden, acts out impulses conventionally repressed. Psychosis certainly produces suffering, but this is a by-product, the result of the clash between the psychotic process and the social order: the power of the latter is such that most people who embark on the psychotic voyage end up as casualties. But psychosis itself, not just in its emblematic form or as a symbol of what is possible, but in its reality – psychosis itself is the opposing principle to order and constraint, it is a genuinely joyous and unappeasedly anarchic transcendence of attempts to force human nature into any particular straitjacket. Psychosis is, therefore, not to be understood as extreme susceptibility to the pathogenic power of modernity, but, rather, as a utopian position, as the way out.

Various problems with all these views have been outlined in the course of this chapter. Those which are shared include a tendency to romanticise schizophrenia, not necessarily over-come by attempting to distinguish between psychiatric patients and an abstract 'psychotic process', alongside a failure to appreciate the concrete suffering experienced by the victims of a psychotic breakdown. In addition, most of the theoretical positions fail to offer guidelines on the distinction between normality and psychosis – on what it is that makes it possible for some people to retain a sense of autonomy and stability whilst others find their selves disappearing all around. It also remains unclear why psychosis, rather than other pathologies of the self, should be the emblem of modern disturbance, unless one is to be content with the view that there is a continuum of disorders of selfhood ranging, in order of severity, from narcissism, through borderline states, to schizophrenia. This position has certain attractions – for instance, it opposes the reification of madness present in psychiatric theory and practice – but it misses the specificity of different responses to social conditions, which may themselves vary from person to person. That is, it makes the social processes that construct the personality too uniform, varying only in severity, hence failing to account for resistance, revolution, or even just some forms of sanity.

It is also uniformly negative about modern society, although the emphasis in *Anti-Oedipus* on the energetic and 'relatively deterritorialising' nature of capitalism partially redresses this point. But what is stressed throughout is the pathogenic tendency in modernity, its disavowal of tradition, stability, nurture and interpersonal support. As Deleuze and Guattari's account makes clear, this is only one side of the equation: along with the disorientation produced by modern capitalism's dismantling of structure and community comes freedom from outmoded shackles, displacement of boundaries that do not serve the interests of production, and, of course, a far wider range of potential satisfactions for personal desires than has ever been available before. And this last point is not a negligible one: if the self is built out of relations with others and with the material world, then the relative richness of possible vessels into which the self can be projected – which can become embodiments of self expression – will substantially influence the complexity and richness of that self. After all, that is partly what artistic creation is about.

This is not meant to be a defence of modernity in every respect. The point here, made previously in Chapter 1, is that ambiguity and ambivalence are precisely the nature of the contemporary environment: it is both exhilarating and disturbing, both enrapturing and unsettling, both exciting and threatening, both the source of gratification and of persecution. The psychotic process, on the other hand, seems locked into the negative term of all these oppositions. The psychotic cannot share in the expansive possibilities of modernity because her or his delirium recognises only the persecutory elements – and the same seems to be true for many of the theorists of postmodern psychosis. Perhaps, in fact, it is postmodernist theory that fails here: unable to conceive of a mode of selfhood that could oppose the fragmenting tendencies of modernity, it dissolves into either a lament for a lost supportive structure – an essentially traditionalist message – or into a paean to nihilistic explosions of desire. Either way, taking the psychotic process or state of mind as the truest expression of the modern condition is a guarantee that only one half of the ambiguity of contemporary experience will be grasped.

Something, too, is neglected about psychosis itself. The pictures painted are too indistinct and partial; some striking phenomenological characteristics of some schizophrenics are abstracted from the mass, highlighted and then seen as emblems of contemporary society. The direction of the argument, however, tends to go the other way round. First comes a view of what is wrong with the social order, then the utilisation of selected elements in psychotic experience to act as case studies of this disturbance. The consequence of this, given the rich pickings to be found in madness, is that almost any critical appraisal of modernity, particularly if it focuses on its disorienting impact, can appear to be supported. Not only is this a poor methodology for the construction of a social theory, it is also an inadequate approach to understanding psychosis. Indeed, no real attempt is being made in any of these theories to determine what the nature of the psychotic process is; the image of the psychotic, in some places romanticised, is simply being used to support particular critiques of the social order – which may or may not be justifiable in their own terms. This makes good polemic, sometimes good poetry, but not good theory.

Presumably, there is some connection between the dominant mode of organisation of society and the kind of psychological states of mind – both balanced and disordered – that it throws up. Presumably, then, modernity does have important and meaningful connections with psychosis, just as it has with narcissism. But, again as with narcissism, the development of some understanding of what these connections might be requires more than a phenomenological juxtaposition: the modern social order is mad, psychotics are mad, therefore psychosis is the modern condition. What is required here is more detail about the nature of the psychotic process and, in particular, about its actual links with social relationships, before it can be used as a form of commentary on contemporary existence. That is, answering the question 'What can be learned from psychosis?' first demands some analysis of what it is that is going on when the psychotic process is operating in people. 'Analysis' here means more than just a statement that, for example, schizophrenia is 'caused' by a genetic predisposition and a precipitating set of social stressors. Rather, it demands an account of what is happening psychologically within the psychotic experience – what it means, what its psychological structure might be, and what psychological processes might be acting. To achieve this, some psychoanalysis is necessary, some account of the dynamics of the psychotic state of mind. This is the topic of the next chapter: to provide a description of some promising psychoanalytic perspectives on psychosis, and only then to ask, what social world is embedded in this?

Chapter 6

Psychotic States of Mind

Recuperating reality

At first glance, one might expect to find a celebration of psychosis in psychoanalysis. In its refusal to recognise the constraints of reality, its externalisation of internal events, its acting-out of desire, psychosis looks like an illustrated history of the unconscious, a material and observable presentation of what can usually be discovered only with enormous effort and expertise. Some psychoanalysts (e.g. Fenichel, 1945) have viewed psychosis as a condition in which the ordinary constraints imposed on unconscious material are given up, with the thought-processes characteristic of psychotic states being in the 'purer' primary-process mode. No negation, no time, no self-other boundary, no experienced contradiction between logically incompatible ideas: these absences define the nature both of the unconscious and the psychotic state of mind. Most significantly, both the unconscious and psychosis are opposed to reality. For the former, reality is that which imposes constraints on the pleasure-seeking urges of the drives, so compelling unhappiness, while for the latter it is that which threatens to invade and demolish the self, enticing, frustrating, persecuting, soul-destroying. The opposition between reality and the unconscious is basic, at least in Freud's view, and has to be negotiated by all humans. But whereas normal and neurotic individuals deal with the threats raised by reality by repressing or sublimating their desires, so that they never stray too far from their unconscious, unacted-upon state, psychotics manage it by wishing away reality itself, by refusing to live in a world that denies and punishes the deepest human impulses.

There is clearly some room in this analysis for the validations of madness seen in the previous chapter. Siding with the unconscious, psychotics could be construed as a revolutionary vanguard: 'say no to reality, let us have the life of the imagination and the repressed potentials of unconscious desire'. As suggested in *Anti-Oedipus*, it could be the neurotic who is more truly to be pitied, the one who has half-noticed the oppressive impact of society but who has not the strength of mind to repudiate it utterly. But this suggests that psychotics have some degree of choice over what they do, or at least that they gain something by losing the world, a suggestion which, by and large, is at odds with the reported experience of psychotic patients themselves. 'The centre of schizophrenia is annihilation,' writes Kovel (1987, p. 336), 'the person becoming schizophrenic remains materially present and conscious, but ceases to be'. This perception, that what occurs in psychosis is a wiping-out of the self rather than a voluntary renunciation followed by transcendence, is the starting-point for most psychoanalytic accounts.

There is no celebration of psychosis in Freudian psychoanalysis; the psychotic state of mind is an escape, a fantastic immersion in unreality as a replacement for the unbearable real reality with which the individual is faced. Schizophrenic psychosis is a severe condition, more severe than neurosis and also more deeply rooted than paranoia, which has its source in repressed homosexuality and which Freud differentiates from schizophrenia on the basis of its fixation points and its mechanism for production of symptoms. Most importantly, whereas paranoia offers some way back to contact with reality through its creation of a coherent alternative conceptual system – the paranoid delusion – schizophrenia is cut off from all organised modes of thought. Paranoia retains the outward form of thought structured according to the reality-principle, but changes its content; schizophrenia, on the other hand, is characterised by the disintegrative process. Thus, in schizophrenia,

> The victory lies with repression and not, as in [paranoia], with reconstruction. The regression extends not merely to narcissism (manifesting itself in the shape of megalomania)

but to a complete abandonment of object love and a return
to infantile auto-erotism. The dispositional fixation must,
therefore, be situated further back than in paranoia, and
must be somewhere at the beginning of the course of
development from auto-erotism to object love. (Freud,
1911, p. 217)

'Somewhere at the beginning', writes Freud, suggesting
somewhere pre-Oedipal, before the entry of the 'third term',
the Symbolic matrix, the organising principles of social being
and belongingness. One marker of the difference between
psychosis and neurosis lies in this early fixation point.
Neurotics suffer from their awareness of the incompatibility
between their desires and what can be tolerated by the social
world – the conflict between the Oedipal impulse to be in
possession of the mother (the other) and the prohibitions
placed on unfettered desire by the father (the law or incest
taboo). Acceptance of the yoke of the father represents
acceptance of the structuring power of social reality – its
ability to constrain the sexuality of the child so that it flows
along socially sanctioned channels. Neurosis has its fixation
point here, in the pain engendered by this repression;
nevertheless, it acknowledges the primacy of society, even if
it cannot cope with the tension this creates. Psychosis, on the
other hand, never gets this far: its fixation point is well before
the coming of society, far back in the two-person self-other
relationship. Indeed, the existence of the other is barely
recognised, for the fixation point hovers around the distinction between I and you, a distinction which schizophrenia
continually disfigures. Freud calls the preponderant neuroses
studied by psychoanalysis the 'transference neuroses', reflecting
the way objects of desire are substituted until they become
acceptable. Psychosis, however, is not really about objects at
all.

In schizophrenia . . . after the process of repression the
libido that has been withdrawn does not seek a new
object, but retreats into the ego; that is to say, that here
the object-cathexes are given up and a primitive objectless
condition of narcissism is re-established. (1915, p. 202)

Hence these are the 'narcissistic neuroses'; they have to do not with the relationship between the individual and the world, but with that between the individual and the self. In the narcissistic neuroses, there is truly no other.

Symington (1985) points out that, in psychoanalytic psycho-therapy, the psychotic transference is characterised by an enormous intensification of emotion and a deep and terrifying fusing of self with other – not just a lack of differentiation, but an I-thou merger with no prospect of separation, no interruption or formation of a discrete consciousness. The psychotic is marginalised, 'outsided' in the sense that she or he never enters the symbolic structures of Oedipus but, *pace* Deleuze and Guattari, this is not experienced as freedom; it rather carries the intense threat of complete destruction and dispersion, of being swallowed up by the unmediated other. 'In the psychotic transference the patient feels overwhelmed and almost suffocated, and cries out to the analyst to free him or her from the situation' (Symington, 1985, p. 233). An unbearable lightness of being indeed: absence of being, absence of the structuring force enabling the emergence of a differentiated self, is experienced not as liberation, but as terrifying vulnerability. It is this that makes reality so devastating to the psychotic. The neurotic has a self, a bounded ego that experiences repression and knows what it has lost. The narcissist, too, has a self, however slippery and empty it may feel, however much in need of bolstering by admiration and megalomania. But the psychotic self has no boundary at all, it flows unstoppably into otherness, its life is drained out from it, its energy dissipated, its coherence a fiction. Consequently, everything that should be outside the self can enter in with no opposition; all those private spaces of the mind which mark the difference of one person from another, myself from yourself – all these can be invaded and lost. Under such circumstances, if desperate steps are not taken quickly to ensure survival of some elemental spark of self, there will be nothing left there that can take any steps at all.

Freud writes that psychosis originates in a conflict between the ego and reality, and presents reality as an unproblematic entity, comprehensible and undeniable.

In a neurosis the ego, in its dependence on reality, suppresses a piece of the id (of instinctual life), whereas in a psychosis this same ego, in the service of the id, withdraws from a piece of reality. (Freud, 1924b, p. 221)

The psychological mechanism at work here is *disavowal* (London, 1973), the renunciation of perception before it can be appropriated in consciousness. However, normal mental life feeds off the interrelationship between inside and outside, self and other; disavowal of the other means that the self collapses. Hence, the withdrawal from, and denial of, reality, leaves an absence which is so terrifying that it has to be covered over – Freud (1924a, p. 215) writes that a delusion can be found 'applied like a patch over the place where originally a rent had appeared in the ego's relation to the external world'. Indeed, all the familiar symptoms of psychosis – particularly hallucinations and delusions – are secondary attempts to make good this rupture by replacing the unbearable reality with a new one, 'a new reality which no longer raises the same objections as the old one that has been given up' (Freud, 1924b, p. 223). Thus, in psychosis the ego is under the sway of the id, reality is ignored for the sake of psychic comfort, accurate perception of the external world is displaced by phantasies from within.

Freud's insight that the first-rank symptoms of schizophrenia can be understood as attempts at restitution, at recuperating reality, is an immensely productive one. Not only can it be applied to the more obvious contents of schizophrenic thought, such as delusions and hallucinations, but it also clarifies the form taken by this thought, particularly its concreteness and muddle over the relationships between words and things. Post-Freudian understandings of the peculiar nature of psychotic words will be returned to below; Freud, however, locates its significance in the context of an hypothesis about the normal relationship between language and the unconscious. What is the difference between a conscious and an unconscious presentation of an idea? 'The conscious presentation comprises the presentation of the thing plus the presentation of the word belonging to it, while the unconscious presentation is the presentation of the thing alone' (Freud, 1915, p. 207).

However, psychotic thinking is characterised by a very peculiar set of links here.

> If we ask ourselves what it is that gives the character of strangeness to the substitutive formation and the symptom in schizophrenia, we eventually come to realise that it is the predominance of what has to do with words over what has to do with things. (1915, p. 206)

Usually, thing-presentations are in the unconscious, and words become attached to them to bring them to consciousness; such, after all, is the therapeutic process of psychoanalysis itself. But in psychosis the thing – the object in all its reality – has been lost, leaving only the word to be clung on to. Psychotic words, therefore, are attempts to reconstitute the things which normally they would signify; they thus cease to be signs and become objects in their own right. What is the psychological mechanism in operation here, how is it that words come to substitute for objects, that the schizophrenic is so concrete in her or his thinking as to mistake the name of the rose for the rose itself? Freud's answer is that the loss of the object is so devastating that the psychotic tries to regain it; but the loss is also so absolute that only the representation of the object can be retrieved. Having the word is better than nothing; the name is at least a reminiscence of the thing.

> It turns out that the cathexis of the word-presentation is not part of the act of repression, but represents the first of the attempts at recovery or cure which so conspicuously dominate the clinical picture of schizophrenia. These endeavours are directed towards regaining the lost object, and it may well be that to achieve this purpose they set off on a path that leads to the object via the verbal part of it, but then find themselves obliged to be content with words instead of things. (1915, p. 209)

Again, this suggests that repudiation of reality is no enviable state of affairs. The psychotic cannot bear reality and so disavows it; but the emptiness produced by the loss of the object is so poignant and painful, that desperate attempts to regain it, to people the mind with a substitutive reality, are undertaken. Sadly, these attempts fail: inside is muddled with outside, anxieties and wishes with perceptions, words are mistaken for things. So the psychotic is trapped, no way forward and no way back.

Laplanche and Pontalis (1973) point out that there are some ambiguities in Freud's account of psychosis as a retreat from reality. This is particularly because of its assumption that an unproblematic perception of reality is possible, and that this plays a balancing or possibly constructing role in the individual's psychic economy. Laplanche and Pontalis note, 'Freud is obliged to make reality play the part of an actual autonomous force, almost as though it was itself an agency of the psychical apparatus' (p. 372). But this straightforward idea of reality as a homogeneous entity opposed to the individual is subverted by Freud's recognition of the complex interweaving of phantasy and perception to be found in psychic life. What is it about reality that is so disturbing to the individual, and what does it actually mean to renounce or disavow this reality? For Freud, disavowal was a defence mechanism particularly associated with fetishism and characteristically directed towards repudiation of the perception of castration. To some extent, then, the reality which the psychotic is denying is biological; but if one recalls that castration anxiety is interlinked with the Oedipus complex, and hence with the founding structures of social organisation (the Oedipus complex being the developmental point at which society enters in to forbid certain biologically possible expressions of the sexual drive), then it appears that what is being denied is the power of social reality to swamp individual desire. More specifically, the disavowal is of sexual difference: rather than recognise the possibility of castration, the psychotic denies what has been seen. This, however, means that the psychotic cannot enter into the position of being either masculine or feminine; and in denying that she or he has gendered status the great sexually dimorphic structures of society have to be renounced as well. Thus, the failure to be able to tolerate a decision about personal status leads to denial of the whole world; if one is unable to take a stance as a particular kind of self in society, then no self is possible at all.

From this discussion it is clear that Freud does not view psychosis as any kind of breakthrough, despite its affinities with the unconscious, but as a form of denial that shuts the individual off from the world, leading her or him to take refuge in imaginary structures, desperately staving off the encroachments of reality. There is nothing to celebrate in psychosis, however symbolic it may seem (to those who, unlike psychotics, are able to use symbols and metaphors); for certain, reality may be awful, but even more so is the loss of any place within it. Delusions and hallucinations express rupture, denial, rents in the fabric of connectedness; all this may also be true of the postmodern environment, but that does not make psychosis a way of dealing with it.

Signifying nothing

The work of Jacques Lacan has been a particularly strong influence on some cultural critics who are concerned to draw out the psychotic possibilities of postmodernism. This is largely because of Lacan's emphasis on representation and on language: the focus on the image and the word are rightly construed as particularly central characteristics of contemporary culture. What Lacan appears to offer is a theory of subjectivity that demonstrates the interweaving of these cultural forces, ideology, and personal life. Such an association has much to recommend it: Lacan's work powerfully registers the impact of many of the most important philosophical and cultural theories of the twentieth century, even if the connections are sometimes obscure and the insights more nebulous than they might at first seem (see Macey, 1988). Additionally, the provocative stance taken by Lacanians on issues of symbolism, social influence and sexual difference have been immensely helpful in advancing debates on politics and personal subjectivity (see Frosh, 1987, 1989; Gallop, 1982).

The concern here, however, is with Lacan's portrayal of psychosis. Frequently, a reference to Lacan accompanies an account of the postmodern condition, with psychosis being used in an illustrative or metaphorical sense; the metaphorical status of the link is then allowed to wither away, so that psychosis *becomes* the contemporary experience. Jameson's (1984) reference to the snapping of the signifying chain in both schizophrenia and modernity is like this: it poignantly links the fragmentation of the postmodern environment (particularly the discontinuity in the temporal past-present-future chain) with the isolated chunks of experience – broken and unrelated signifiers – that characterise schizophrenia. But this is illustration, not illumination: it accompanies a fluid text and makes resonant links, using the image of schizophrenic fetishising of the individual word as an emblem of postmodernism's manipulation of the empty signifier. This, however, is itself a postmodernist strategy: a complex concept is concretised, taken out of context, juxtaposed with a different entity from another context, and then the two are treated as the same – interchangeable and indistinguishable in what they represent. What is gained here is a set of enticing metaphors; what is lost is the specificity of the original concept. Here, that means a failure to explore the nature of the Lacanian psychotic.

What is this nature? It is linked to the contrasting orders of the Imaginary and the Symbolic, the former characterised by a romanticised and narcissistic phantasy of wholeness and ego-integrity, the latter by the organised structures of culture and language – the Oedipal order – that shatters this phantasy by driving a wedge between self and other, between desire and its object. To some extent, as Finlay (1989) shows, it is the Lacanian gloss on narcissism and its relation to the Imaginary that is most impressive as a portrayal of contemporary cultural and personal experience – the fragmentation implicit in language is counterposed to the Imaginary wholeness apparently guaranteed by the appearance of the mirror image, which is in fact an immersion in narcissism. But while it is true, as described in Chapter 5, that the concept of narcissism informs a potent lament for the lost content of the self, and that the regressive longing for a more familiar and predictable order of things can be theorised as a refusal of the Symbolic in favour of an Imaginary return to the womb, there is another process at work that links very forcefully with the Freudian insights described above. Refusal of the Symbolic is, like the refusal of the Oedipal father in which it is embedded, a refusal to recognise the causal powers of reality; it is, therefore, more of a psychotic than a straightforwardly narcissistic process.

Lacan himself says, 'When it comes to the psychotic subject, if he loses the realisation of the real, he doesn't find any imaginary substitute. That is what distinguishes him from the neurotic' (Lacan, 1975, p. 116). More fully:

> it may be the case that the specific structure of the psychotic should be located in a symbolic unreal, or in a symbolic unmarked by the unreal. The function of the imaginary is to be located somewhere entirely different. (p. 117)

The psychotic process is not, therefore, one to be sought in the realm of the Imaginary order. Indeed, it does not consist of the acceptance of any structured order at all; rather, its connection is with the Symbolic, but only as a negation of that crucial state of being. What, then, is the source of psychosis, what does it 'mean'? Lacan's clarifying move here is to tighten up Freud's concept of disavowal by employing a new but related term, *foreclosure*.

> It is in an accident in this register [of the signifier] and in what takes place in it, namely, the foreclosure of the Name-of-the-Father in the place of the Other, and in the failure of the paternal metaphor, that I designate the defect that gives psychosis its essential condition, and the structure that separates it from neurosis . . . For the psychosis to be triggered off, the Name-of-the-Father, *verworfen*, foreclosed, that is to say, never having attained the place of the Other, must be called into symbolic opposition to the subject. (Lacan, 1977, pp. 215, 217)

Foreclosure is something like disavowal, but refers very specifically to the apparatus of the Symbolic order; it is repudiation in the context of the necessity of entering into relations with the structures of cultural reality. Its operation is at the stage before the perception of the repudiated thing is even registered; it is different from negation because it is as if the foreclosed thing had never existed. And what is it that is foreclosed, what lost, ghostly signifier is left to haunt the world outside the psyche, no home to call its own? The clue is the Name-of-the-Father. Laplanche and Pontalis (1973) spell it out: for Lacan, foreclosure is 'a primordial expulsion of a fundamental "signifier" (e.g. the phallus as signifier of the castration complex) from the subject's symbolic universe' (p. 166). Again, 'foreclosure consists in not symbolising what ought to be symbolised (castration): it is a "symbolic abolition". Whence Lacan's formula for the hallucination . . . ". . . what has been foreclosed from the Symbolic appears in the Real"' (p. 168).

Repudiation of castration, foreclosure of its signifier – symbolic abolition of the phallus. This is not just repression, but a forbidding of entry of the signifer even into the unconscious, so that the only way it can appear is as hallucinated in 'the Real', that is, outside of symbolisation. But repudiation of the phallus, foreclosure, bars entry to the Symbolic; it is this that is at the heart of psychosis. The Symbolic is necessary 'for socially relating to others in a mature and mutual dependency as opposed to solipsistically retreating from them into asociality and amorality' (Finlay, 1989, p. 60). It is the necessary condition for language, for the activation of cultural and interpersonal positioning. As with the traditional formulations of the Oedipus complex, the Symbolic does represent a constraint on the possibility of fulfilment of desire; but without it there can be no bounded sense of I and you, no social existence or linguistic connection with others. Refusal of the Symbolic means refusal of the social; moreover, there is no location of the individual 'subject' in any meaningful array of symbols. The world swims away, the defining structures of subjectivity are renounced. Certainly this means that the psychotic is not pinned down by Oedipus – Deleuze and Guattari are right about that. But this does not make the psychotic process one which is filled with free desire and revolutionary energy. Outside the Symbolic is absence, is a desperate retreat into the Imaginary, is a failure to relate – is an experience of possession by concrete objects which cannot be symbolised, which are persecutory and paranoid, which are full of threat and totally out of control. The desperation of the self faced with this experience might well be postmodern in its form and intensity; but psychosis is a very specific as well as a

very deeply disturbing state of mind, for Lacanians as much as
for Freudians. It is characterised by the terrifying emptiness of
exclusion from the main defining axes of human subjectivity.

Inside and out

Psychotic thought processes, rather than the fantastic content
of psychotic thought, have increasingly become the primary
concern of post-Freudian analysts working with schizophrenic
patients. This is particularly the case for Kleinians, but other
analysts have shared their interest in what it is that the
psychotic does with thoughts as well as words, that makes
them come out so different from the thoughts and words of
other people. The answer to this question is given most
powerfully in terms of psychological processes which are
shared with those employed by non-psychotic individuals –
especially young children – but which are found in psychotic
patients in an extreme and devastatingly unbalanced form.
Because these are, generally speaking, processes concerned
with externalisation and internalisation – with projection,
introjection and projective identification – their exaggeration
is accompanied by a confusion of inside and out, leading to
that specifically psychotic tendency to relate to others as if they
were phantasies deriving from the self.

Searles (1961) describes how the paranoid schizophrenic is
dominated by persecutory introjects (internalised objects)
which are in fact representatives of repressed and projected
qualities of her or his own.

> The patient lives chronically under the threat not only of
> persecutory figures experienced as part of the outer world,
> but also under that of introjects which he carries about,
> largely unbeknown to himself, within him. These are
> distorted representations of people which belong, properly
> speaking, to the world outside the confines of his ego but
> which he experiences . . . as having invaded his self. These,
> existing as foreign bodies in his personality, infringe upon
> and diminish the area of what might be thought of as his
> own self – an area being kept small, also, by the draining off,

into the outer world, through projection, of much affect and ideation which belongs to the self. (p. 100)

The narcissist is aware of how hard the battle is to sustain a remnant of selfhood in the face of the draining and persecutory unsupportiveness of the environment; the self of the psychotic, however, has been infiltrated by this environment so completely that there is nowhere left to turn. The self is alien to itself, because its contents are experienced as parasitical: there are 'foreign bodies' in exactly the place where one should feel most at home. In addition, the things which should be there – the psychotic's own mental contents – have been projected into space, so that they are now left, forlorn and anchorless, to float around in the outside world, attached in bits and pieces to unsympathetic or ghostly objects. But it is not just mental contents (thoughts and fantasies) which suffer in this way: it is also mental *processes*, the activities of the mind which really constitute thinking. Searles uses Hartmann's (1939) idea of dedifferentiation here: what schizophrenic fragmentation entails is largely a loss of differentiated psychological functions, for example of phantasy or memory. Thus, the patient cannot tell the difference between thought and reality, leading to the concreteness which Freud remarked upon so clearly. So, too, does the psychotic fail to distinguish trivial from important events, and also to know when a new person is not someone 'doing a take-off' of someone previously known. The threatening end point of this is that the patient 'will cease to exist as a human individual' by being reduced to 'an animal, a dead person, or an inanimate object' (Searles, 1961, p. 108); the process by means of which this happens, is a destruction of the ability to sustain integrated and functional thoughts.

In a slightly later article, Searles (1963) identifies the components of the 'transference psychoses' encountered during therapy. He notes that the transference in psychotic patients 'is expressive of a very primitive ego-organisation, comparable with that which holds sway in the infant who is living in a world of part-objects, before he has built up an experience of himself and of his mother and other persons around him' (p. 183). This means that the normal transference of psychotic patients is one in which the analyst is experienced as a maternal object from which the patient is not yet distinct: the patient is constantly confusing her or his self with that of the analyst, rather than, as is more conventionally the case in the transferences of other patients, confusing the analyst with other external objects. In addition to this problematic state of affairs, the picture can be clouded still further by the operation of transference psychoses, defined by Searles as 'any type of transference which distorts or prevents a relatedness between patient and therapist as two separate, alive, human and sane beings' (p. 190). Searles lists four varieties of transference psychosis, plus a 'delusional identification' state in which the patient identifies with a distorted vision of the analyst. These four varieties all in one way or another express the desperation of the patient's attempt to become a separate person; most poignantly, the last of them shows both sides of the therapeutic struggle. This is the type of transference in which,

the deeply and chronically confused patient, who in childhood had been accustomed to a parent's doing the thinking for him, is ambivalently (a) trying to perpetuate a symbiotic relationship wherein the therapist to a high degree does the patient's thinking for him, and (b) expressing, by what the therapist feels to be sadistic and castrative nullifying or undoing of the therapist's efforts to be helpful, a determination to be a separately thinking, and otherwise separately functioning, individual. (p. 206)

The most painful component of this partially restitutive attempt is that the patient, trying to become someone separate, does so by attacking the therapeutic process, by nullifying the advances which are made, or attacking the attempts of the analyst to understand and enhance the patient's own interpretive capacities. Indeed, this is almost bound to be the case, given the phenomenology of psychosis. The patient experiences her or himself as unbounded, invaded by persecutory elements from the outside world, into which the fragments of the self have also been dispersed. The struggle of the psychotic patient is to regroup these fragments by drawing a boundary between inside and out, even if this means finding a fantastic content for the self, and an hallucinated one for

external reality. The analyst's empathic interpretations, know-
ledgeable statements and penetrative insights, are perceived as
further manifestations of the violating power of the outside, of
the inability of the patient to maintain a private mental space
of her or his own. Thus it goes on, one step forward and two
steps back: psychosis perpetuated by the very acts dedicated to
its undoing.

This is not the place for a discussion of the therapeutic
strategies available when working with psychotic patients.
Suffice it to say that Searles reads the evidence above to
mean that it is necessary to first enable the patient to discover
a sense of containment through an accepting, symbiotic
relationship with the analyst/mother before interpretive work
can be undertaken – a point of view opposed by Kleinians in
much the same terms as were rehearsed in the debate over the
treatment of narcissism. What is more central here is Searle's
appreciation of the crucial role played in psychosis of
projective and introjective processes that split the contents of
the self, but that also demolish many of the mental functions
which are normally taken to be specific characteristics of
human psychology. These are, of course, not just rational
functions: the whole of psychoanalysis attests to the inade-
quacy of a simple rational/irrational marker for the difference
between sanity and madness. Rather, the psychotic is cut off
not just from rationality, but also from the normal irrationality
of the human subject: the unconscious organisation of desire,
the workings of repression and sublimation, the life of
integrated, wish-fulfilling phantasy. Instead, there is a loss of
self and of the contents and apparatus of the mind; in their
place is a fragmentary world of partial objects and autonomous mental mechanisms, dedifferentiated and dysfunctioning.

Kleinians have taken this set of perceptions still further.
Beginning with Klein's (1946, 1957) ideas on the operation of
paranoid-schizoid phantasies in early life and on the disruption
to normal splitting that can be caused by excessive envy which
is unmodified by a supportive environment, Kleinians have
been concerned with psychosis as the paradigmatic instance of
uncontrolled splitting and projective processes. These processes
have both constitutional and environmental sources. Klein
(1957) states very clearly that the determinants of splitting and

projection lie in constitutional envy and that when such envy is held in too great a quantity (that is, when the death drive is too strong), an exaggerated splitting may occur. This means that the normal division of the object into good and bad elements changes into one between extremely idealised and denigrated components – the idealised and persecutory objects. If this excessive constitutional envy is not ameliorated by a particularly containing and responsive environment, the conditions for a permanent and violently opposed splitting of the psyche are laid down. Rosenfeld (1952) notes that internalised (introjected) idealised as well as persecutory objects contribute to increasing the severity of the super-ego, thus generating a tendency towards extremely punitive self-judgements with consequent anxiety and guilt. According to Rosenfeld, the roots of the psychotic state can to a considerable extent be found here: the inability of the patient to withstand these feelings,

> causes the projection of the self, or parts of the self containing the internalised object, into external objects. This results in ego splitting, loss of the self and loss of feelings. At the same time a new danger and anxiety situation develops which leads to a vicious cycle and further disintegration. Through the projection of the bad self and all it contains into an object, this object is perceived by the patient to have changed and becomes bad and persecuting itself. (p. 29)

What is particularly feared is the 'forceful aggressive re-entry of the object into the ego'; a defence against introjection results, which has the further consequence of retaining the persecutory object in the external world whilst doing nothing to ease the aggression from within. 'In the process,' Rosenfeld notes, 'the ego is in danger of being completely overwhelmed, almost squeezed out of existence'.

It is not just an inability to find the boundary between self and other which is being emphasised in this account, but the way a devastated inner world is seen reflected in the external world, which indeed has contributed through its own negativity to the perpetuation of despair. It is characteristic of the

Kleinian approach that the original source of destructiveness is assumed to be internal – constitutional envy, in Klein's own theory. This interacts with an uncontaining real environment to produce the spiralling mechanisms of splitting and persecution which have been described. The social world is secondary in this theory, but it does have a real part to play in managing the child's destructiveness and hence mollifying the anxiety to which this destructiveness gives rise. In normal development, this interchange between inside and out does not only occur in phantasy: it is a real exchange around patterns of feeding and childcare, in which the parents stay more-or-less calm, whole and gratifying for the child. For the psychotic, however, the internal and external worlds are for ever bound up together in a punitive and persecutory cycle, so that even the somewhat tenuous hold on reality which, according to Kleinians, is the normal state of affairs, slips away. All alone, far away from real object relationships, the psychotic's inner and outer worlds are indistinguishable, each a morass of unintegratable phantasy.

Much of this inner-outer confusional exchange is mediated by an exaggerated use of projective identification, perhaps the most powerful psychic mechanism described by Kleinians and also one which is deeply evocative of many of the psychosis-like phenomena of contemporary culture. Laplanche and Pontalis (1973, p. 356) define projective identification as 'a mechanism revealed in phantasies in which the subject inserts his self – in whole or in part – into the object in order to harm, possess or control it'. Rosenfeld (1971) provides a more detailed account that refers closely to the psychotic experience.

> 'Projective identification' relates first of all to a splitting process of the early ego, where either good or bad parts of the self are split off from the ego and are as a further step projected in love or hatred into external objects which leads to fusion and identification of the paranoid parts of the self with the external objects. There are important paranoid anxieties related to these processes as the objects filled with aggressive parts of the self become persecuting and are experienced by the patient as threatening to retaliate by forcing themselves and the bad parts of the self which they contain back again into the ego. (p. 117)

What is central to this concept is the idea that it is not just feelings or emotions that are projected, but 'parts of the self', inserted into the external object partly for protection and partly as an aggressive act. The consequence of this, as the material from Searles has already suggested, is that the external object becomes infused with persecutory content. The *paranoid* nature of the ego-object relationship is thus given by the way the experienced destructiveness of the object is in fact a product of the subject's inner destructiveness, which has been put into the object as an available vessel. This object may indeed have some persecutory qualities of its own, which will make matters worse, but even if this is not the case it will be experienced negatively, because it is carrying the subject's own aggression and envy. Where the external object can manage the situation by receiving the subject's aggression without retaliation – as in good mothering and psychotherapy – the destructiveness will gradually be ameliorated. When, on the other hand, the object is itself so vulnerable or envious that it retaliates and rejects the subject – as in the parenting conditions giving rise to psychosis – a vicious cycle of splitting, projective identification, terror of introjection of the persecutory object, and more splitting will ensue. The final consequence of such a cycle is a psyche which has been blown to pieces.

Rosenfeld (1971) distinguishes between a small number of different kinds of projective identification, with differing forms and functions in the therapeutic situation. The major distinction is between 'projective identification used for communication with other objects and projective identification used for ridding the self of unwanted parts' (p. 120). The former is obviously the more positive form: in infancy it is a normal mode of non-verbal communication with the mother, whose task it is to contain, mollify and restore the projected elements of the self so that they can be integrated into the infant's incipient ego. The analytic task in this situation is exactly the same. The psychotic patient projects impulses and parts of the self into the analyst, who reduces their terror by surviving the attack contained in their destructiveness without retaliating, and by making them intelligible through interpretation. Rosenfeld comments,

This situation seems to be of fundamental importance for the development of introjective processes and the development of the ego: it makes it possible for the patient to learn to tolerate his own impulses and the analyst's interpretations make his infantile responses and feelings accessible to the more sane self, which can begin to think about the experiences which were previously meaningless and frightening to him. The psychotic patient who projects primarily for communication is obviously receptive to the analyst's understanding of him. (p. 121)

Whilst there is still an effort at communication, however rudimentary and infantile may be the psychological processes involved, there is still some chance: if the analyst can survive and make sense of the projected missiles emanating from the patient's self, something restorative can be provoked. Other forms of projective identification, however, are less benevolent. When it is used for denial of psychic reality,

> the patient splits off parts of his self in addition to impulses and anxieties and projects them into the analyst for the purpose of evacuating and emptying out the disturbing mental content which leads to a denial of psychic reality. As this type of patient primarily wants the analyst to condone the evacuation process and the denial of his problems, he often reacts to interpretations with violent resentment, as they are experienced as critical and frightening since the patient believes that unwanted, unbearable and meaningless mental content is pushed back into him by the analyst. (p. 121)

So far, so bad: projective identification is at best a crude mechanism for communication which, because of its primitive passion and inherent destructiveness, is more likely to be met with aggressive repudiation than with toleration and support. But worse than this is the form of projective identification in which the destructive and destroyed components of the self are dumped on the external object not so that they can be worked with, but so that they can be removed from circulation – evacuated. As will be seen below, this is the form of projective identification regarded by Bion as most characteristic of the psychotic thought process: an emptying out of undigested and intolerable material, leaving the self drained of living content. However, even this is not quite the worst: Rosenfeld describes a variant, but common, form of projective identification in which the patient attempts to omnipotently control the analyst through the projective process. Such a patient experiences her- or himself as having entered into the analyst; this means not only that the self-other boundary has been obscured, produc- ing anxieties about the loss of the self, but also that the patient phantasises the analyst as having been infected with her or his own madness.

> In this form of projective identification the projection of the mad part of the self into the analyst often predominates. The analyst is then perceived as having become mad, which arouses extreme anxiety as the patient is afraid that the analyst will retaliate and force the madness back into the patient, depriving him entirely of his sanity. At such times the patient is in danger of disintegration. (p. 122)

The self-object distinction has been obliterated, the power to think abstractly is lost, symbolic equation (in which symbols are taken for concrete entities) predominates, metaphor is mistaken for reality. The patient's absorption in the analyst can be experienced as an aggressive and parasitical object relationship, in which the patient feeds off the analyst, using the analyst's aliveness as a means for survival in the face of the patient's own inner deadness. Whilst other forms of object relationship are possible in psychosis (for instance, what Rosenfeld refers to as 'delusional' ones), it is this penetrative, aggressive deadness that is perhaps the most characteristic and demoralising element in the psychotic process. Everything with which the psychotic comes into contact is drained of life, its goodness sucked out of it, its nurture poisoned. The uncon- trollable, envious destructiveness of the psychotic, uncontained in infancy, out of control in adulthood, is survived only at the cost of an active disintegration of the self and projection of the remnant bits. Fusion with the analyst allows the patient some sense of omnipotent, if parasitical, mastery; separation when

the analyst clarifies boundaries or makes penetrative interpretations, releases a huge rush of spoiling aggression. The
consequence of all this for the psychotic patient is that the
object as well as the self seems mad.

The mechanisms of projective identification have been
described in some detail as they are central to many
contemporary psychoanalytic accounts of the psychotic process. In particular, projective identification as evacuation and
omnipotent projective identification operate to expunge the
intolerable anxiety, born of envy, from the psychotic mind. But
this results in the mind itself being expunged, so producing an
experience of weirdness in which everything is penetrated by
everything else, boundaries are lost, and the world is filled with
aggressive bits of self and object, in mutual, parasitical
harassment.

Annihilatory pieces

The most evocative psychoanalytic portrait of this psychotically deconstructed self is that painted by Bion. According to
Bion (1967, p. 37), there are four essential features of
schizophrenic personalities.

> First is a preponderance of destructive impulses so great that
> even the impulses to love are suffused by them and turned to
> sadism. Second is a hatred of reality . . . Third, derived
> from these two, is an unremitting dread of imminent
> annihilation. Fourth is a precipitate and premature forma-
> tion of object relations, foremost amongst which is the
> transference, whose thinness is in marked contrast to the
> tenacity with which it is maintained.

The terms of this list are worth noting: destructiveness, hatred
of reality, dread, tenacious but superficial clinging to the
object. This is a description of an organism whose roots are
slipping from the soil, earth crumbling all around, with
nothing on which to take hold. And as it slips, so Bion
suggests, it attacks all potential growth, all health, all meaning: it is as if it strives to destroy meaning itself before

meaninglessness withers it from within. The phenomena of psychosis – concreteness, attacks on language, destruction of thought and the links between thoughts, projective identification, envy and paranoia – these are seen by Bion as the central elements of a mind that cannot bear so much reality.

As described earlier, Lacan places a refusal to enter the Symbolic, and hence to become a fully acculturated language-user, at the heart of psychosis. Despite his very different terminology and theoretical orientation, Bion's view is somewhat similar to this. Extending Segal's (1957) suggestion that psychotic thinking is marked by the use of symbolic equations instead of symbols (and hence by the symbol/reality confusion which recurs so regularly in discussions of schizophrenia), Bion (1970, p. 68) portrays the language of psychosis as an arena in which there is no employment of words as symbols, indeed no employment of symbols at all. Rather, the reduction of words to things, noted by Freud, indicates the severity of the boundedness of the psychotic's thought-processes, the way mental space is filled with concrete objects which cannot be worked on in any creative way, but can only, at best, be evacuated like faeces. Underlying this inability to use language fluidly and creatively is a drying-up of thought, or, rather, an active attack on thinking that precludes any 'learning from experience' – under some circumstances, a kind of foreclosure, a destruction of all meaningful links. This is, indeed, the schizophrenic rubble, the splitting of signifiers until they become isolated aggressive bits, useable only as missiles, experienced internally as faecal bricks. No dreaming is possible, because dreaming is linked to reverie and the toleration of disturbing thoughts and phantasies; no digestion of experience is allowed, just denial and a foreclosed shutting-out of emotion. Overall, this means that psychotic thought is reduced just to projective identification in Rosenfeld's second sense – thoughts as projectiles, the thinking apparatus itself extruded from this desperate being.

For Bion, psychotic thought is characterised by the domination of what he calls 'β-elements' and the relative weakness of the 'α-function' which should be employed to work on these elements. Bion gives the clearest extended account of the nature of β- and α-elements and α-function in *Learning from*

Experience (1962). Here, it is made clear that β is the undigested, raw material of experience, concrete blocks which must be worked on and shaped by α-function if they are to be integrated into the thinking and creative (dream) life of the person. Alpha-function itself is the process of thought, that which transforms experience from one mode to another – that which makes experience digestible.

> Alpha-function operates on the sense impression, whatever they are, and the emotions, of which the patient is aware. In so far as α-function is successful α elements are produced and these elements are suited to storage and the requirements of dream thoughts. If α-function is disturbed, and therefore inoperative, the sense impressions of which the patient is aware and the emotion which he is experiencing remain unchanged. I shall call these β-elements. In contrast with the α-elements, the β-elements are not felt to be phenomena, but things in themselves. (p. 6)

Beta-elements should not be confused with unconscious thoughts: indeed, one of the damaging aspects of the failure of α-function is that it results in a loss of the ability to differentiate between conscious and unconscious thought – 'α-function is needed for conscious thinking and reasoning and for the relegation of thinking to the unconscious when it is necessary to disencumber consciousness of the burden of thought' (p. 8). Beta-elements cannot be made unconscious, because they cannot be worked on at all, except as missiles, as the content of projective identifications centred on the denial of reality.

> They are the objects that can be evacuated or used for a kind of thinking that depends of the manipulation of what are felt to be things in themselves as if to substitute such manipulation for words or ideas. (p. 6)

They just sit there, great toads that they are, intermittently leaping whole into space, devouring consciousness, devouring links with others, devouring thought. Is this foreclosure again?

Domination by β-elements, if it does occur in psychosis, certainly seems to represent an inability to recognise experience, let alone learn from it – without α there can be no symbolisation, no dreaming, and no relationship of self with self or other. Instead, the self functions as a series of automatons, with bits of thought evacuated whole through projective identification, rather than being lived or fully experienced. Moreover, the normal process of transmuting β-elements can under some circumstances, particularly when envy is too strongly operative, be actively reversed, destructively attacking α-function, divesting α-elements of all that makes them useable in thought, producing a psychic world full of the infamous Bionian 'bizarre objects' – split off aspects of the psyche, full of persecution and hate.

Bizarre objects are fragments of the self, tiny bits of mind which are deliberately disconnected to make them less vulnerable to attack from the persecutory object. However, because they have themselves become infused with destructiveness and because they are subject to projective identification, the creation of bizarre objects produces a phenomenological universe which is desperately concrete and dangerous, but also mysterious and confusing. Bizarre objects are not the same as β-elements, for 'the bizarre object is β-element plus ego and superego traces' (p. 26). But it seems that psychotic thought is permeated by both. The collapsing psychotic psyche, full of β, attacks its own creative functioning, splits into minute fragments and evacuates itself and its objects through projective identification, following a perversely inverted consumption-production-consumption cycle run wild. At the source of this cycle is envy and hate, unmitigated by successful containment in a calm mothering experience. Too much hatred, too powerful an inner sense of annihilation and death, leads to attacks on α-function, on thought and meaning. Not only do raw β-elements remain untransfigured, blocking digestion, but what meaning there is in experience is actively attacked by the psyche. Bizarre objects are the enveloped containers of the residues of meaning, filled now with destructiveness and persecution. The self is in bits, making up an ersatz world in which reality is masked by the completely unreal, in which meaning is constantly destroyed.

In practice it means that the patient feels surrounded not so much by real things, things-in-themselves, but by bizarre objects that are real only in that they are the residues of thoughts and conceptions that have been stripped of their meaning and ejected. (Bion, 1962, p. 99)

Bion (1962) refers to the inability of the psychotic to dream as an instance of the lifelessness of psychotic existence – there is nothing to differentiate sleeping from waking states. But the attack on meaning goes further than this. Placing its origins in the envious attack on the maternal breast, Bion (1967) describes how the psychotic's destructiveness is turned against anything which might resemble, or become, a self.

Identical attacks are directed against the apparatus of perception from the beginning of life. This part of his personality is cut up, split into minute fragments, and then, using the projective identification, expelled from the personality. Having thus rid himself of the apparatus of conscious awareness of internal and external reality, the patient achieves a state which is felt to be neither alive nor dead. (p. 38)

More foreclosure comes into play as the psychotic splits ego and objects, anything that 'would make him aware of the reality he hates' (p. 47). Everything is attacked, the ravaging paths of hate consuming ego, object, thought, links between thoughts – anything that connects, makes sense, provides contact with reality, suggests meaning. These things represent to the psychotic the possibility of total annihilation by the force of her or his hatred and envy; so not perceiving is essential, and because of that the apparatus of perception itself must go. But this perpetuates the spiral: no sense can be found anywhere, the psychic universe consists only of persecutory bizarre objects and β-elements, leading to more devastation and more intense annihilatory panic. Thus, the psychotic patient strives to create more meaninglessness, through hallucinations or perhaps catatonic withdrawal – attacks on everything until no further threat can be perceived, until the whole of experience has been foreclosed.

There is, however, some thought in psychosis. Bion (1962) discusses the formation of a 'β-screen' to replace the usual α-screen marking the contact-barrier between conscious and unconscious. This β-screen, confused and partial though it is, has some purpose and evokes emotions in the analyst – usually alarm or intense anxiety. But the central issue about thought, according to Bion, is that it arises as a necessary response to the frustrations induced by reality: its crucial, defining aspect is to make frustration tolerable, to mediate the actual situation of the desire-full human individual. Thought, therefore, predates thinking: that is, because thoughts occur, a thinking apparatus has to be constructed to deal with them. It is here that psychosis and normality begin to blur. Bion (1962) proposes that the thinking apparatus is built on the model of the digestive system; in the case of the psychotic, this model is taken literally, so that thoughts get turned into faeces, denuded of all that is good and expelled from the body/psyche as waste. And what differentiates psychotic from non-psychotic thought is not really all that much: just an ability to tolerate frustration sufficiently to be able to modify it. Thoughts are experienced as bad, because they represent a need which is unfulfilled; they must therefore be removed.

> They can be got rid of either by evasion or modification. The problem is solved by evacuation if the personality is dominated by the impulse to evade frustration and by thinking the objects if the personality is dominated by the impulse to modify the frustration. (p. 84)

The concreteness of psychotic thought is this first response, evasion resulting in an inability to symbolise and a domination by 'undigested facts' (Bion, 1965, p. 41). There is no modification of inner or outer reality, but its conversion into an uninvested commodity, a totally concrete yet meaningless no-thing.

Bion's work has been immensely and widely influential, particularly amongst followers of the post-Kleinian school of which he was a member. Its primary contribution is to provide an account of psychotic thought-processes that explains the intensity of the psychotic terror whilst also linking it with normal psychological processes. However, this is perhaps only one element in the appeal of this work. Bion's construction of a new language for psychoanalysis, his relative abstraction and his adoption of a mathematical-sounding superstructure for his theory, has given his approach the flavour of difficulty and challenge that always serves to whet the appetite of those who, when faced with the apparently inexplicable, seek something formal, rigorous and seemingly scientific. Yet, mixed with this seeming-scientism is a fluidity of therapeutic description which is constantly moving and startlingly acute, alongside an evocation of the psychotic experience which is unmatched by any other theoretician. Perhaps, indeed, this is the telling point in Bion's attractiveness. Like Lacan's, Bion's writings are not always, or even usually, easily decipherable. But, again as with Lacan, if one gives oneself up to the flow of his texts, if one becomes absorbed in the language of β and α, bizarre objects and projective identification, thought-apparatus and evacuation, then what occurs is a spinning in the head that is both insightful (it does have content, it is not completely mad) and evocative. Everything turns around, thoughts come before thinking, blocks of experience before the perceptual apparatus; the self can be in bits, experienced as outside itself, words are things and things are bodily parts. All this is a theory, ostensibly explaining the psychotic condition; but it *is* the psychotic state as well.

And so the danger recurs. When one is faced with an inexplicable reality, mysterious theories can be very attractive. But not all people are as capable of retaining their rigour of thought in the face of this as are the originators of the best of these theories. The works of Lacan and Bion have content, but they also have style, and this style is so closely congruent with psychotic thought itself that it can sometimes replace the content to become all that there is. When that occurs meaning slips away, metaphor becomes reality, the word replaces the thing. The poetry of Lacan and Bion, of psychoanalysis itself, evokes psychosis with great poignancy and power; but it is crucial that this evocation does not also obscure the suffering reality of the schizophrenic condition.

Postmodernism, concrete consumption and reverie

In postmodernist theory, it is the surface-centredness of
modernity which is emphasised, the way things – goods,
objects, people – represent nothing other than their appearance, do not hang together as part of some greater whole. This
makes them, in some important ways, interchangeable: one
thing seeps into another, every boundary is crossed, everything
can be taken apart and reconstructed in another order. If there
is nothing essential 'inside', no specific signified tied to a
particular signifier, then no one thing is more important or
more real than any other. The self, too, is such a commodity,
signifying nothing; more fully, it is a fiction generated as a
protection against recognition of the fragmentary nature of
experience. In Lacanian psychoanalysis, this lack of integration is taken to be the truth of the human subject: full of desire,
all of it based on absence and lack, the subject hunts around
for a semblance of order that will make it possible to survive
the confusion of inner and outer reality. Alighting, in the
mirror phase, on the ego, the appearance of integration is
achieved: but it is only appearance, the mirror image has
nothing behind it except a thin band of reflective material.
What looks like depth is taken for reality, but it is a fraud; the
self is an Imaginary construct, produced to make narrative
sense of each individual's personal history. In the more
revolutionary, or at least anarchic, eyes of schizoanalysis, the
dismantling of the self is seen as a political and philosophical
imperative, a way of challenging totalising theories and
appeals to human nature, a subversive deconstruction of all
claims to authority and power.

The most extreme varieties of theoretical antagonism
towards the ego may seem more like (sometimes self-aggrandis-
ing) polemic than honest investigation, but, as usual, they do
contain a strong element which is evocative of real experiences
and perceptions actually had by people living in the conditions
of modernity. Indeed, this is probably one source of their
appeal. It is not just that the libertarianism of, for instance,
Anti-Oedipus provides an imaginative escape for individuals
frustrated by the difficulty of living an orderly life in the face of
the ravaging confusion which is to be found in the contempor-

ary urban environment. It is also that the argument against the primacy of the self reflects an internal struggle which is a genuinely shared, objective function of modern life. This struggle is, in a way, that of staving off madness: it is the struggle towards the construction of an autonomous and honest mode of personal being, even if this can never be an absolute phenomenon. The difficulties encountered in this struggle are very pronounced, so much so that they drive some people into psychosis and they make the phenomenology of that state comprehensible to all of us. In addition, it is almost certainly the case, as schizoanalysts, Laingians and others have shown, that many instances in which there is an apparently 'normal' adoption of selfhood are actually cases of pathological conformism, in which the actual needs and desires of the subject are displaced by a socially acceptable veneer. Indeed, it is possible that this is an element in all adjustment: such would be the implications of much social theory and also of many mainstream psychoanalytic positions – Freudian and Winnicottian, for example, as well as Lacanian. The question is, however, whether this element of conformism and alienation should be interpreted as an indicator of the basically unintegratable nature of human desire, the fundamental irreducibility of the subject to any kind of self. The celebrants of psychosis discussed in Chapter 5 take the psychotic process to be revolutionary because it shatters the image of naturalness that surrounds the bourgeois self and reveals that underneath there is bubbling, exciting confusion. Psychosis is taken as a revelatory state: what it reveals is how fake our ordinary, alienated experiences of our selves actually may be.

Clearly, one attraction of this position is that many people do indeed experience themselves as alienated – and that this experience is especially widespread under the conditions of modernity. However, the psychoanalytic work described in this chapter makes it apparent that, far from being a liberated state, the dissolution of selfhood characteristic of psychosis is deadeningly disempowering and frantically terrifying. As the self disappears in destruction and rage, the subject tries desperately to fill the space which remains. The vacuum is clearly abhorrent; that way nothing lies. What this suggests, therefore, is that it is not the dissolution of self embodied by psychosis that is the state towards which liberational struggles should aspire, but the construction of new selves which are not so alienated, not so conformist or pained. The psychoanalytic work on narcissism and psychosis reveals that this is a deeply problematic task under social conditions that militate against the formation of the kinds of interpersonal relationships required to achieve this, but that does not alter the argument that self-construction should dominate over even the most penetrating and poetic of deconstructionist assaults.

There is no necessary essentialism in this point of view, no assumption that each of us has a pre-given self which is uniquely ours from birth, its properties waiting only to be expressed, not made. All the deconstructive critiques of post-structuralism and much of psychoanalytic theory have shown the difficulties with that suggestion (see Banton *et al*, 1985): the self is not a once-and-for-all possession but is something constructed during development, taking as its elements the bits and pieces of internal and external experience. Nevertheless, even if the self is not 'essential', it may be real: just because something is constructed, with difficulty and mishap along the way, it does not mean that it does not exist. The achievement of some sense of self may be an end rather than a beginning; psychoanalysis reveals how difficult achievement of this end can be. In addition, one attraction of the deconstructionist theories is that they show how fragile is the nature of this social construction which we know as the self: underlying it are disconnected forces and disparate bits of desire. But the lesson of psychosis seems to be that without this hard-won end, this fragile construction of self, there is no core to human subjectivity.

Deleuze and Guattari (1972) focus on the productivity of the unconscious, the way 'desiring-machines' produce desires, for their portrayal of the dynamic of the modern psyche. Postmodernist theory as a whole, however, has been more concerned with consumption, with the idea that the world is full of objects which are made in some mysterious way, their productive processes unknown and unfathomable, which do not connect and which are created to fill unreal needs. As relationships with material objects form an important element in people's encounters with their environment, in a culture where nothing hangs together, where consumption is itself an alienated force, having no bearing on anything 'real', the experience of individuals will be similarly fragmented and superficial, made up of unintegratable bits. The enormity of unmarked space in some postmodernist architecture, or the juxtaposition of contradictory styles in buildings, commodities and dress – these are the reflections in popular culture of the growing, more fundamental awareness that there is no particular truth, either of the subject or of the 'object', no way of being that makes any particular sense.

All this chimes in strongly with the Lacanian discourse of the snapping of the signifying chain, resulting in a schizophrenic rubble of unrelated signifiers, each expressing only itself. It is also present in the Bionian discourse of β-elements and bizarre objects: the former undigested, thing-like turds of experience, the latter split-up bits of the self, invested with persecution and hate. Bion even offers some hints as to what the relationship might be between postmodernist patterns of consumption and a state of mind dominated by β-elements. He suggests that the patient who is filled with envy and hatred pursues material things with a desperate and insatiable hunger, but that this pursuit, because it is an attempt to fill an unfillable void, is never satisfying.

> He feels surrounded by bizarre objects, so that even the material objects are bad and unable to satisfy his needs. But he lacks the apparatus, α-function, by which he might understand his predicament. The patient greedily and fearfully takes one β-element after another apparently unable to conceive of any activity other than introjection of more β-elements. (Bion, 1962, p. 11)

Is this the mad extreme of consumption? All things interchangeable, nothing fickle, fallow, spare; just objects in the severest sense. Could this be what the postmodernists are getting at? A world of such β-consumption, such eating up of relationships, such nothingness: this is what Bion portrays as the psychotic state of mind. It is reminiscent of the total interchangeability and insignificance of the postmodern universe, the way nothing can be converted into symbolic form, because nothing has representational status. The two, psychosis and consumption-based postmodernism, will also go together, if it is in fact the case, as seems likely, that much of what we take to be our self is built up from our relationships with material objects, and therefore that the more stable and meaningful these objects are, the more secure and integrated will be the self (see Miller, 1987; Lasch, 1979). But it does also raise some further questions: for instance, is this really an ordinary state in postmodern society? Is consumption really as meaningless as this?

The resonances undoubtedly exist between postmodernist conceptions of culture as unremitting alienated consumption, and psychoanalytic portrayals of the inner world of the psychotic patient. In this connection, it is worth recalling that nowhere in psychoanalysis, neither in Lacan nor in Bion, is psychosis held up as the healthy mode of contemporary experience. It remains pathological. On the other hand, and notwithstanding the genuine 'psychotic' parallels, psychoanalysis makes no easy assumption of the pathology of all of modern or postmodern culture, or of a 'truth of the subject' that is inevitably psychotic at its core, all other states being defences against this truth. What psychosis is about, according to psychoanalysts of all persuasions, is a refusal of experience – foreclosure, attacks on α-function. In material terms, this can be seen as an attitude towards consumption which is certainly postmodernist because it refuses to make sense of things, but which is pathological precisely because of this refusal, or inability – because instead of using consumption as a means to feed the self, to create some inner identity, it leaves everything undigested, to be evacuated whole. This bears on the extreme deconstructionism mentioned above, which constitutes a major false element in the postmodernist position: the assumption that just because the self is constructed it must be unreal. To recapitulate: the self is indeed a 'construct'; the realisation of this is one of the major advances of the modern movement. It is made up of bits of experience, of relations with others, of internalisations of social processes – of material which is ingested, digested, made part of the psychic body. From this the inner being of each person takes shape. The self is, therefore, distinctively social rather than inherited in a straightforwardly essentialist way – but it is a real locus of ➤ experience and symbolisation nevertheless. What is shown by the accounts of psychosis to be found in the works of the psychoanalysts discussed here, in their different ways, is what happens when this reality is rejected, when the self really does become a fragment, a manifestation of unreality. It is not the struggle to be a self under postmodern conditions which is psychotic, but the relinquishing of that struggle.

Bion emphasises that hate is the root of the psychotic evil. The infant's intense hatred and envy of the breast is projected outwards; the failure of the receiving object to take hold of this hatred, to mediate it and allow recuperation, results in the tremendous inner tension and despair that causes psychotic splitting and the evacuative projective identification which goes along with it. This projective identification destroys all meaning, all curiosity and knowledge, all learning from experience – the kind of learning from which the self is constructed. Opposed to this scenario, however, is the mechanism which Bion proposes as the route to health, both in the original developmental situation and in the analytic encounter. This route consists in the successful containment of the infant's or patient's aggression, in a holding container – in the end, a person – that allows its expression but mediates and moderates its destructive power. The process of such containment, or, rather, the stance or attitude making this process possible, is described by Bion by the term, 'reverie'. This was first mentioned in Chapter 3, but can now be returned to more formally.

> Reverie is that state of mind which is open to the reception of any 'objects' from the loved object and is therefore capable of the reception of the infant's projective identifications whether they are felt by the infant to be good or bad. In short, reverie is a factor of the mother's α-function. (Bion, 1962, p. 36)

It is a kind of dreaming state, a receptiveness to all experience, to everything that the child can offer; this is, too, as Symington (1985) glosses, the state of receptivity to be sought by the analyst, basically an openness to being changed by the patient's experience.

> A conscious state of not-knowing underpinned by a preconception stance seems to be what Bion recommends. Through the analyst's being a container . . . it is possible for a transformation to occur in the patient, from a means of communicating through projective identification to one where there are dream thoughts. This explains the paradox that when a patient has a dream, a phantasy or a thought about a particular thing it means that the thing is already within manageable proportions and can be so dreamed, phantasised or thought about. What had been got rid of through projective identification has now been reintrojected in a modified form, so can be dreamed about. (pp. 293–4)

Taking in, holding, making sense, giving back – this is the process of containment resulting from the state of reverie. From the point of view of the infant or patient, the experience of such a containment is of having one's fragmented self, with all its destructive elements, accepted, tolerated and made manageable, alongside an awareness that this beneficial cycle arises from the presence of a holding, reliable and patient other.

It is this kind of other which is continually undermined in contemporary culture: it is hard, if everything is continually slipping away, to be stable long enough to offer containment. No reverie occurs where roots are gone. But even leaving aside the general applicability of postmodernist descriptions of consumption and of culture, not everyone is frankly psychotic, even if all of us have our psychotic moments and parts. First, it seems that even in a disintegrated world, people are able to make some sense of their patterns of consumption, to partially define themselves through what they do, what they have and how they use it – and what relationships they make (e.g. Miller, 1987). Secondly, the fragmentation can be repelled. Integration, movement from paranoid-schizoid to depressive positions, symbolisation, reverie: there are plenty of prospects here, not for some total health or perfect state of well-being, for these undoubtedly are fictitious Imaginaries, but for islands of creativity, for dreams, for resistance. Psychoanalysis offers accounts of psychosis which are congruent with postmodernist descriptions of contemporary culture; but it also conceptualises psychosis as a state of suffering and distress, as a pathological state which can be resisted and moderated through therapy. In so doing, psychoanalysis rejects the picture of psychosis as a summary image of contemporary life: the struggle to become a self may be more difficult under contemporary conditions, but it is still possible and worthwhile. This conclusion, of course, says as much about deterministic postmodernist theories of culture as it does about psychotic states of mind.

Conclusion: The Crisis of Identity

Identity crisis

Under modern conditions, the construction of a self is a struggle at best won only provisionally and always entailing expenditure of considerable amounts of psychological energy. Contemporary cultural theories and psychoanalysis, with their differing but intersecting planes of investigation, attest to the intensity and pain of this struggle, which is opposed at every point by the structure and dominant forces of modernity. The consequence of this state of affairs is that the self is never secure, requires unremitting protection and nurture, is always in danger of being undermined, of withering away or exploding into nothingness. With every move that is made, every step taken to encounter or withdraw from the world, some new turmoil is embraced, some new source of fragmentation unearthed. The problematic of modernity for its individual subjects lies largely in precisely this condition: that there is no absolute stability, no still point from which bearings can be taken.

Such is the 'identity crisis' of individuals in contemporary society. Culture itself has no clear identity, unless one allows its amorphism to be so described; it is characterised by rootlessness, instability, rapid transition from one state to the next, one fetish to another. Communicational immediacy, interchange of ideas and style without establishment of a frame within which to view and understand them (yesterday the East, today Africa – as these cultures become increasingly distorted by western depredations, so they are romanticised by the mystical soul-seekers of the West): under these conditions, discovery of one's own roots, one's own centre of consciousness and growth, becomes an impossible task. Consequently, the instabilities of society are internalised as instabilities of the self, the rapidity of external change is experienced as inner turmoil, the fragmentation of the cultural environment becomes a buzzing and booming confusion in the head. Something in this is exhilarating: plugging into the voices of the world produces an hallucinogenic consciousness of great excitement and passion, and introduces new sounds and rhythms which can be genuinely stimulating and creative. This is part of the up-side of modernity: that the constraints of the past, the narrowness induced by geographical and familial fixedness, can be transcended through exposure to a huge range of differing attitudes, expectations, cultural practices and modes of social organisation. Perceiving how others live their lives can make it possible to acquire new insights and perspectives on how one lives one's own.

But this can happen only in the context of some stability of identity, the possession of some notion of what constitutes the central aspects of one's experience. Otherwise, the expansion of consciousness which is possible in the modern world is like the filling and popping of a balloon: tantalisingly it grows and grows, becoming more and more exciting; but it is so full of air that its borders break and all that is left is the withered skin. Thus, exposure to the lives of others is reduced to voyeurism, producing either a desultory sense of entertainment or a deeply distorting envy. Disparate traditions are collapsed into their common denominators: the music of Africa, for example, thrills while it is unfamiliar, but quickly is assimilated to western beats and background sounds. Cultural distinctions are celebrated and sought out, but are experienced as if they were all the same. Absorption of one another's heritage means a three-minute encounter with the songs and calendar that may once have provided the binding forces around complexly knit societies. Understanding where once we came from means tracing a family tree and naming your child after the earliest uncovered ancestor – or, alternatively, some mythical goddess of the soil.

Modernist and postmodernist accounts of contemporary culture have many shared elements that converge on the portrait given above. Both identify the exhilaration of modernity with its ebullience of content; both, too, show how this can result in an uncontrollable spiralling of perception, denying individuals any clear consciousness of order or stability. Both, therefore, attest to the problems posed to the identity of the modern subject – to the self as an internal structure supplying integrity and depth to each person's encounters with the world. Where they differ fundamentally, however, is in the attitude adopted towards this difficulty, in the analytic value-system within which the descriptive account takes place. The opposition, discussed throughout this book, is between those who celebrate the dissolution of the self and those who mourn it; correlatively, it is between those who see the contemporary denial of order and integrity as a method of disavowing the ideological constraints of bourgeois society, and those who see it as a despairing abrogation of the responsibility for resistance in the face of the explosive power of modern patterns of domination.

Despite the variety of readings of selfhood, ego-function and developmental history which can be found in the psychoanalytic literature, there is a strong shared theme that places a premium on the construction of internal integrity. As a shorthand, one can call this the necessity for the achievement of selfhood: some inner, balanced order that allows emotion to be experienced and desire expressed within a context of stability of personal boundaries and an openness to relationships with others. The exact content of this selfhood would be seen very differently by adherents of the different approaches described in this book and some, notably those following Lacan, would be antagonistic to this terminology of the self and to any suspicion of valorisation of egoic control over the dissensions and contradictions of unconscious desire. As has been argued earlier, there is much to be gained from taking such points of view seriously, particularly because they provide a powerful counterweight to idealising tendencies, which can be found in the work of some of the more self- or object-oriented theorists. However, as the discussion of psychosis made clear, even amongst these opponents of the ego there are few who celebrate the dissolution of the whole structure of the psyche: for them, psychosis is a process of shutting out experience that denies the subject any encounter with reality, relegating her or him to impotent brawls with hallucinated desires. For most psychoanalysts, the argument against dissolution is even stronger. This is obvious in the case of self-theorists and object-relations theorists, and also in the more classically-oriented contemporary work of Chasseguet-Smirgel and Grunberger. But it is also true for those celebrants of unconscious impulse, the Kleinians and their allies, for whom the achievement of an integration of experience with a large space for unconscious irrationality, is the central concern of developmental and therapeutic progress. Giving up the battle for this kind of 'self' results in a phenomenological world full of ghosts, as discarded and repudiated bits of inner life fill the external void, persecuting and betraying the subject at every move.

Psychoanalysis, therefore, endorses the struggle for self, an endorsement which on the whole brings it closer to modernist than to postmodernist approaches. This does not, however, mean that there is any assumption that this struggle will be easily won. Quite the contrary: if anything, psychoanalysis implies that the conditions required to guarantee stability of selfhood are so stringent that they could barely ever be met in their entirety within any imaginable social order. These conditions, as revealed in the literature on narcissism and psychosis, centre on the requirement that the early developmental environment of the child shall be one in which her or his aggressive loves and hates can be contained and managed through the actions and mediations of an accepting other – a 'container' stable, strong and integrated enough to take in and hold these passionate intensities without being broken itself. What this in turn requires is the existence of objects – humans, usually parents – who are stable and centred in their own selves, who are not desperate to defend against their own narcissistic wounds or so disintegrated that the demands of the child and their own inner despair merge into a boundary-less, persecutory universe. The givers of self must have self; yet, as described throughout this book, the conditions that character-ise modernity make the achievement and preservation of self endlessly problematic. The high standards which psychoana-lysis sets, combined with the particularly unsettling nature of contemporary life, seem to make asseveration of the impor-tance of construction of a stable self academic: however important it might be, it does not seem possible to achieve it.

Reverie and resistance

This gloomy conclusion is not easy to dispute. One reason why it makes sense to portray people's experience in terms of 'identity crisis' is that modern individuals are subjects within a culture which is in part constituted by its ability and tendency to produce precisely that experience. It is in the nature of modernity to provoke crises of identity: that is what modernity is about, that is what supplies its immense energy and productiveness. Old rules have constantly to be re-written, as nothing can be taken for granted, no previous identity accepted unquestioned; without 'identity crisis' there would be no momentum, no ever-stirring, never-ceasing change. But this is also what produces the terror endemic to modernity, as the rapidity and brutality of social and material transformation leaves few areas of certainty or arenas in which individuals can control their own destiny; more metaphysically, there is never any way of knowing for certain where we are or what constitutes our worth. Modernity displaces, disturbs, deconstructs and redeploys; that is its nature, and any social structure with a nature like that must produce a fragmenting environment for personal life.

Despite the persuasive logic of this argument, modernism has always held that there is a possibility of self-assertion in the face of the real disarray produced by modern conditions, with artistic creation being a particularly clear example of what such self-assertion can mean. In that instance, it is as if the inner experience of identity crisis is circumvented through the creation of some external object which embodies the inner disturbance and so makes it possible to take up a stance towards it, to have a relationships with it out of which some emotional and perhaps intellectual sense can be made. Psychoanalytic practice can be construed similarly: the individual's unconscious impulses are externalised, often through projection or projective identification, and thus can become the objects of analysis in the psychoanalytic dialogue. The artistic 'object' is there replaced by a more immediately personal one, but in each case the mechanism is rather like the objectification process described in Chapter 1. Something internal and partially unknown is externalised and worked

on until it has recognisable shape, then it is taken back inside
and appropriated as a representation or embellishment of
'identity', a path to the construction of a more integrated
and elaborated self.

But we are caught in a vicious cycle here. What makes this
objectification process possible, according to psychoanalysis, is
the presence of a containing other, one who through achievement of a state of reverie can hold the distress of the subject,
modify and ameliorate it, and allow it to be re-appropriated in
this worked-through, more tolerable form. However, as noted
above, the conditions of modernity seem particularly badly
designed for the promotion of reverie: such a balanced and
open mental state can only be built on the basis of the sort of
stable self which is belied by the whole 'identity crisis'
dynamic. In addition, there is the argument to contend with
that these apparent deepenings of self and discoveries of
autonomy and identity are actually fictitious, imaginary
representations of what one might like to be or, more
perniciously, internalisations of the ideological directives of
the dominant social order. It should be said that this is always
a possibility and often a deep danger, but the difficulty of
distinguishing between real and ideological developments of
the self does not mean that such a distinction is meaningless.
The most important example here, and again one which has
been an implicit theme in much of this book, is the dichotomy
(worked out in the discussion of Grunberger's theory of
narcissism) between regressive and realistic solutions to
psychological conflict – to the crisis of identity. In the
discussion of narcissism, the comparison was between 'narcissistic' solutions built out of a regressive desire to return to the
pre-natal state, and 'Oedipal' solutions forged through encounters with reality. Characteristics of the former solution
were denial of contradiction, desire for a state of conflict-free
bliss, disavowal of anality, pursuit of purity, and absorption in
a fantasy of completeness. Such lifeless but rigid Imaginary
states can easily be seen to be characteristic of fascism and
other ideologies opposed to the heterogeneity and contradictions of modernity – ideologies that protect people from the
realities of the world by denying those realities, by offering a
framework of total predictableness and by brooking no

opposition. These clearly are the kind of solutions which are distortions of reality, and they produce selves which on the surface may appear strong (because their affiliations and interpretations of events are so certain, and because they gain emotional support from the group-cohesive structures needed to preserve this certainty), but which are actually despairing attempts to stave off the dissolution threatened by the contradictoriness and challenge of the modern world.

Progressive, 'Oedipal' solutions to the crisis are characterised by an engagement with reality of a particular kind. This is that along with the expression of desire there is an acknowledgement of conflict – of the conflict between what is desired and what can be achieved, and also of the conflict between differing positions and possibilities. Implicit in this is a recognition of heterogeneity: conflict is wished away in narcissistic solutions by straightforward denial – alternatives do not exist; Oedipal solutions engage with the conflict and allow internal changes to occur as a result of it. In the paradigm example of the Oedipus complex, the boy acknowledges the reality of the father's power, responding to it by channelling his own desires differently and by internalising the attributes of the father as a series of possibilities for himself. In its raw form, of course, this too is an ideological representation of reality: boys are privileged over girls, repression is theorised as a necessary condition for social survival. It is not, however, the details of this that are relevant here (see Frosh, 1987, for a discussion), but the general structure of the Oedipal encounter. The important point is that it is an encounter with otherness: whereas regressive solutions see and hear no evil, because they deny the existence of anything which does not chime in with their phantasy-structure, progressive, 'Oedipal' solutions are based on the premise that otherness exists and that its constraints and possibilities need to be explored.

This argument also offers some hints to ways of approaching the vicious cycle described above, in which reverie is deemed impossible so no stability of self can ever be found. One characteristic of the theories described throughout this book, mentioned in the Introduction, is that they favour the broad sweep of culture over the specifics of experience of particular groups. This has the advantage of allowing them to make

generalisations of wide potential applicability, drawing attention to the core characteristics of contemporary experience
without the necessity for qualification of everything being said.
But that is also a limitation of this approach: not only is this
kind of cultural (and psychoanalytic) theory often intensely
ethnocentric, generalising possibly mistakenly from a particular variety of western experience to the whole of modernity,
but it also misses the specific differences between subgroups
within western society itself. The most important of these are
obviously minority ethnic groups and women, whose own
experiences of modernity are mediated and infiltrated by
particular patterns of oppression not necessarily theorised in
the general accounts of modern culture. This obviously may
make these theories more limited in their generalisability than
they might suppose: even though many elements of modern
experience will be common to all groups, those which are not
might turn out to be highly significant. Whether Nazism is
understood from a German or Jewish perspective makes a
considerable difference. Conversely, the existence and progress
of specific groups of this kind suggests something else about the
possibilities for achievement of a secure self. Both feminist and
black racial-consciousness movements, despite their limitations
and occasional regressive tendencies (see Wolfenstein, 1989),
have produced alterations in people's understanding of
themselves and others at both an intellectual and emotional
level, and have to some extent generated real material changes
in the standing and relationships of women and black people
themselves. One of the ways in which this has been achieved is
through patterns of identification in which those who struggle
against oppression, from however partial a basis, are seen by
other members of their groups and indeed sometimes by
outsiders, as expressing elements of personality and selfhood
which they can admire and which resonate with internal
processes of their own. Thus, the movements themselves reveal
new insights about the social order and the strengthening of
individual selfhood and 'identity' which is derived from them
can become the starting-point for a beneficial cycle of
externalisation of desire, struggle and re-appropriation of a
strengthened self.

The general point derived from this is as follows. If modernity was monolithic, it might indeed be the case that there was no space for resistance to its power and no possibility for achievement of a secure self that might make such resistance possible. But modernity is not monolithic: it is precisely its nature that it is made up of fragments, of contradictory forces, elements and groups of elements. Progressive solutions to the crisis of identity recognise this, absorb the reality of contradiction and conflict, and provide kernels of identification and challenge that encourage and support people to face this reality. The fragments of self with which each of us faces the world may not be easy to reconcile with one another or forge into a whole, but they may nevertheless be recoverable from the potential dissolution with which they are faced.

References

ANDERSON, P. (1984) 'Modernity and Revolution', *New Left Review*, 144, pp. 96–113.

ARCHARD, D. (1984) *Consciousness and the Unconscious* (London: Hutchinson).

BADCOCK, C. (1983) *Madness and Modernity* (Oxford: Basil Blackwell).

BANTON, R., CLIFFORD, P., FROSH, S., LOUSADA, J. and ROSENTHALL, J. (1985) *The Politics of Mental Health* (London: Macmillan).

BARRETT, M. and McINTOSH, M. (1982) *The Anti-Social Family* (London: Verso).

BARTHES, R. (1977) *Image-Music-Text* (London: Fontana).

BAUDRILLARD, J. (1976) 'Symbolic Exchange and Death', in J. Baudrillard, *Selected Writings*, (Cambridge: Polity Press, 1988).

BAUDRILLARD, J. (1979) 'On Seduction', in J. Baudrillard, *Selected Writings* (Cambridge: Polity, Press, 1988).

BERMAN, M. (1982) *All That is Solid Melts into Air* (London: Verso, 1983).

BERMAN, M. (1984) 'The Signs in the Street', *New Left Review*, 144, pp. 114–123.

BERNAUER, J. (1987) 'Oedipus, Freud, Foucault: Fragments of an Archaeology of Psychoanalysis', in D. Levin (ed) *Pathologies of the Modern Self* (New York: New York University Press).

BETTELHEIM, B. (1983) *Freud and Man's Soul* (London: Fontana, 1985).

BION, W. (1962) *Learning from Experience* (London: Maresfield).

BION, W. (1965) *Transformations* (London: Maresfield).

BION, W. (1967) *Second Thoughts* (London: Maresfield).

BION, W. (1970) *Attention and Interpretation* (London: Maresfield).

BROMBERG, P. (1982) 'The Mirror and the Mask: On Narcissism and Psychoanalytic Growth', in A. Morrison (ed) *Essential Papers on Narcissism* (New York: New York University Press).

BROWN, N. (1959) *Life against Death* (Middletown, Conn.: Wesleyan University Press).

CHASSEGUET-SMIRGEL, J. (1975) *The Ego Ideal* (London: Free Association Books, 1985).

CHASSEGUET-SMIRGEL, J. (1984) *Creativity and Perversion* (London: Free Association Books, 1985).

CHODOROW, N (1978) *The Reproduction of Mothering* (Berkeley: University of California Press.

CIXOUS, H. (1976) 'The Laugh of the Medusa', in E. Maks and I. de Courtivon (eds) *New French Feminisms* (Sussex: Harvester Press).

CUNNINGHAM, R. (1986) '"True" and "False" Creativity?', *Free Associations*, 7, pp. 117–123.

DELEUZE, G. and GUATTARI, F. (1972) *Anti-Oedipus: Capitalism and Schizophrenia* (New York: Viking).

DEWS, P. (1989) 'From Post-Structuralism to Postmodernity', in L. Appignanesi (ed) *Postmodernism: ICA Documents* (London: Free Association Books).

EAGLETON, T. (1986) *Against the Grain* (London: Verso).

ECO, U. (1989) *Foucault's Pendulum* (London: Secker and Warburg).

EICHENBAUM, L. and ORBACH, S. (1982) *Outside In . . . Inside Out* (Harmondsworth: Penguin).

ERNST, S. and MAGUIRE, M. (eds) (1987) *Living with the Sphinx* (London: the Women's Press).

FAIRBAIRN, W. (1944) 'Endopsychic Structure Considered in Terms of Object Relationships', in W. Fairbairn, *Psychoanalytic Studies of the Personality* (London: Routledge and Kegan Paul, 1952).

FENICHEL, O. (1945) *The Psychoanalytic Theory of Neurosis* (London: Routledge and Kegan Paul).

FINLAY, M. (1989) 'Post-Modernising Psychoanalysis/Psychoanalysing Post-Modernity', in *Free Associations* 16, pp. 43–80.

FOUCAULT, M. (1967) *Madness and Civilisation* (London: Tavistock).

FOUCAULT, M. (1972) 'Preface', in G. Deleuze and F. Guattari, *Anti-Oedipus: Capitalism and Schizophrenia* (New York: Viking).

FREUD, S. (1911) 'Psychoanalytic Notes on an Autobiographical Account of a Case of Paranoia (Schreber)', in S. Freud, *Case Histories II* (Harmondsworth: Penguin, 1979).

FREUD, S. (1914) 'On Narcissism', in S. Freud, *On Metapsychology* (Harmondsworth: Penguin, 1984).

FREUD, S. (1915) 'Papers on Metapsychology', in S. Freud, *On Metapsychology* (Harmondsworth: Penguin, 1984).

FREUD, S. (1920) 'Beyond the Pleasure Principle', in S. Freud, *On Metapsychology* (Harmondsworth: Penguin, 1984).

FREUD, S. (1923) 'The Ego and the Id', in S. Freud, *On Metapsychology* (Harmondsworth: Penguin, 1984).

FREUD, S. (1924a) 'Neurosis and Psychosis', in S. Freud, *On Psychopathology* (Harmondsworth: Penguin, 1979).

FREUD, S. (1924b) 'The Loss of Reality in Neurosis and Psychosis', in S. Freud, *On Psychopathology* (Harmondsworth: Penguin, 1979).

FREUD, S. (1925) 'Negation', in S. Freud, *On Metapsychology* (Harmondsworth: Penguin, 1984).

FREUD, S. (1926) 'Inhibitions, Symptoms and Anxiety', in S. Freud, *On Psychopathology* (Harmondsworth: Penguin, 1979).

FREUD, S. (1930) 'Civilisation and its Discontents', in S. Freud, *Civilisation, Society and Religion* (Harmondsworth: Penguin, 1985).

FREUD, S. (1933) *New Introductory Lectures on Psychoanalysis* (Harmondsworth: Penguin, 1973).

FROMM, E. (1970) *The Crisis of Psychoanalysis* (Harmondsworth: Penguin).

FROSH, S. (1987) *The Politics of Psychoanalysis* (London: Macmillan).

FROSH, S. (1989) *Psychoanalysis and Psychology* (London: Macmillan).

GALLOP, J. (1982) *Feminism and Psychoanalysis* (London: Macmillan).

GLASS, J. (1987) 'Schizophrenia and Rationality: On the Function of the Unconscious Fantasy', in D. Levin (ed) *Pathologies of the Modern Self* (New York: New York University Press).

GREENBERG, J. and MITCHELL, S. (1983) *Object Relations in Psychoanalytic Theory* (Cambridge , Mass.: Harvard University Press).

GRUNBERGER, B. (1979) *Narcissism: Psychoanalytic Essays* (New York: International Universities Press).

GRUNBERGER, B. (1989) *New Essays on Narcissism* (London: Free Association Books).

GUNTRIP, H. (1973) *Psychoanalytic Theory, Therapy and the Self* (New York: Basic Books).

HARTMANN, H. (1939) *Ego Psychology and the Problem of Adaptation* (New York: International Universities Press, 1958).

HEBDIGE, D. (1988) *Hiding in the Light* (London: Routledge).

HIRST, P. and WOOLLEY, P. (1982) *Social Relations and Human Attributes* (London: Tavistock).

JACOBY, R. (1975) *Social Amnesia* (Sussex: Harvester Press).

JAMESON, F. (1984) 'Postmodernism, or the Cultural Logic of Late Capitalism', in *New Left Review*, 146, pp. 53–93.

KERNBERG, O. (1970) 'Factors in the Psychoanalytic Treatment of Narcissistic Personalities', in A. Morrison (ed) *Essential Papers on Narcissism* (New York: New York University Press).

KERNBERG, O. (1974) 'Further Contributions to the Treatment of Narcissistic Personalities', in A. Morrison (ed) *Essential Papers on Narcissism* (New York: New York University Press).

KERNBERG, O. (1975) *Borderline Conditions and Pathological Narcissism* (New York: Jason Aronson).

KHILSTROM, J. and CANTOR, N. (1984) 'Mental Representations of the Self', in L. Berkowitz (ed) *Advances in Experimental Social Psychology*, Vol. 16 (New York: Academic Press).

KLEIN, M. (1946) 'Notes on Some Schizoid Mechanisms', in M. Klein, *Envy and Gratitude and Other Works* (New York: Delta, 1975).

KLEIN, M. (1955) 'The Psychoanalytic Play Technique', in M. Klein, *Envy and Gratitude and Other Works* (New York: Delta, 1975).

KLEIN, M. (1957) 'Envy and Gratitude', in M. Klein, *Envy and Gratitude and Other Works* (New York: Delta, 1975).

KOHUT, H. (1966) 'Forms and Transformations of Narcissism', in A. Morrison (ed) *Essential Papers on Narcissism* (New York: New York University Press).

KOHUT, H. (1971) *The Analysis of the Self* (New York: International Universities Press).

KOHUT, H. (1977) *The Restoration of the Self* (New York: International Universities Press).

KOHUT, H. and WOLF, E. (1978) 'The Disorders of the Self and Their Treatment: An Outline', in A. Morrison (ed) *Essential Papers on Narcissism* (New York: New York University Press).

KOVEL, J. (1978) 'Things and Words: Metapsychology and the Historical Point of View', in J. Kovel, *The Radical Spirit* (London: Free Association Books, 1988).

KOVEL, J. (1980) 'Narcissism and the Family', in J. Kovel *The Radical Spirit* (London: Free Association Books, 1988).

KOVEL, J. (1982) 'Values, Interests and Psychotherapy', in J. Kovel, *The Radical Spirit* (London: Free Association Books, 1988).

KOVEL, J. (1984) *White Racism* (London: Free Association Books, 1988).

KOVEL, J. (1986) 'Marx , Freud and the Problem of Materialism', in J. Kovel, *The Radical Spirit* (London: Free Association Books, 1988).

KOVEL, J. (1987) 'Schizophrenic Being and Technocratic Society', in D. Levin (ed) *Pathologies of the Modern Self* (New York: New York University Press).

LACAN, J. (1975) *The Seminar of Jacques Lacan, Book I (1953–4)* (Cambridge: Cambridge University Press, 1988).

LACAN, J. (1977) 'On a Question Preliminary to any Possible Treatment of Psychosis (1955–6)', in J. Lacan, *Ecrits: A Selection* (London: Tavistock).

LAING, R. (1959) *The Divided Self* (Harmondsworth: Penguin).

LAING, R. (1967) *The Politics of Experience* (Harmondsworth: Penguin).

LAPLANCHE, J. and PONTALIS, J.-B. (1973) *The Language of Psychoanalysis* (London: Hogarth Press).

LASCH, C. (1979) *The Culture of Narcissism* (London: Abacus).

LASCH, C. (1984) *The Minimal Self* (London: Picador).

LERNER, M. (1986) *Surplus Powerlessness* (Oakland, CA: Institute for Labor and Mental Health).

LEVIN, D. (1987) 'Clinical Stories: A Modern Self in the Fury of Being', in D. Levin (ed) *Pathologies of the Modern Self* (New York: New York University Press).

LINDNER, R. (1954) *The Fifty-Minute Hour* (London: Free Association Books, 1986).

LONDON, N. (1973) 'An Essay on Psychoanalytic Theory: Two Theories of Schizophrenia', in P. Buckley (ed) *Essential Papers on Psychosis* (New York: New York University Press, 1988).

LYOTARD, J.-F. (1979) *The Postmodern Condition* (Manchester: Manchester University Press, 1984).

LYOTARD, J.-F. (1989) 'Defining the Postmodern', in L. Appignanesi (ed) *Postmodernism: ICA Documents* (London: Free Association Books).

McROBBIE, A. (1989) 'Postmodernism and Popular Culture', in L. Appignanesi (ed) *Postmodernism: ICA Documents* (London: Free Association Books).

MACEY, D. (1988) *The Contexts of Jacques Lacan* (London: Verso).

MAHLER, M., PINE, F. and BERGMAN, A. (1975) *The Psychological Birth of the Human Infant* (New York: Basic Books).

MARCUSE, H. (1955) *Eros and Civilisation* (Boston: Beacon Press, 1966).

MEISSNER, W. (1979) 'Narcissistic Personalities and Borderline Conditions', in A. Morrison (ed) *Essential Papers on Narcissism* (New York: New York University Press).

MILLER, A. (1979a) 'Depression and Grandiosity as Related Forms of Narcissistic Disturbances', in A. Morrison (ed) *Essential Papers on Narcissism* (New York: New York University Press).

MILLER, A. (1979b) *The Drama of Being a Child* (London: Virago, 1987).

MILLER, D. (1987) *Material Culture and Mass Consumption* (Oxford: Basil Blackwell).

MITCHELL, J. (1982) 'Introduction I', in J. Mitchell and J. Rose (eds) *Feminine Sexuality* (London: Macmillan).

MORRISON, A. (ed) (1986) *Essential Papers on Narcissism* (New York: New York University Press).

NEWMAN, M. (1989) 'Postmodernism', in L. Appignanesi (ed) *Postmodernism: ICA Documents* (London: Free Association Books).

REICH, A. (1960) 'Pathologic Forms of Self-Esteem Regulation', in A. Morrison (ed) *Essential Papers on Narcissism* (New York: New York University Press).

RICHARDS, B. (1989) *Images of Freud* (London: Dent).

RIEFF, P. (1959) *Freud: The Mind of the Moralist* (Chicago: University of Chicago Press, 1979).

ROSENFELD, H. (1952) 'Notes on the Psychoanalysis of the Superego Conflict of an Acute Schizophrenic Patient', in E. Spillius (ed) *Melanie Klein Today, Volume 1: Mainly Theory* (London: Routledge, 1988).

ROSENFELD, H. (1971) 'Contribution to the Psychopathology of Psychotic States: The Importance of Projective Identification in the Ego Structure and the Object Relations of the Psychotic Patient', in E. Spillius (ed) *Melanie Klein Today , Volume 1: Mainly Theory* (London: Routledge, 1988).

RUSTIN, M. (1982) 'A Socialist Consideration of Kleinian Psycho-analysis', *New Left Review*, 131, pp. 71–96.

SANDLER, J. (1983) 'Reflections on Some Relations between Psycho-analytic Concepts and Psychoanalytic Practice', *International Journal of Psychoanalysis*, 64, pp. 35–44.

SEARLES, H. (1961) 'Sources of Anxiety in Paranoid Schizophrenia', in P. Buckley (ed) *Essential Papers on Psychosis* (New York: New York University Press, 1988).

SEARLES, H. (1963) 'Transference Psychosis in the Psychotherapy of Chronic Schizophrenia', in P. Buckley (ed) *Essential Papers on Psychosis* (New York: New York University Press, 1988).

SEDGWICK, P. (1982) *Psychopolitics* (London: Pluto Press).

SEGAL, H. (1957) 'Notes on Symbol Formation', in H. Segal, *The Work of Hanna Segal* (London: Free Association Books, 1986).

SYMINGTON, N. (1985) *The Analytic Experience* (London: Free Association Books).

TAUSK, V. (1933) 'On the Origin of the "Influencing Machine" in Schizophrenia', in P. Buckley (ed) *Essential Papers on Psychosis* (New York: New York University Press, 1988).

WHITE, M. (1980) 'Self Relations, Object Relations and Pathological Narcissism', in A. Morrison (ed) *Essential Papers on Narcissism* (New York: New York University Press).

WINNICOTT, D. (1950) 'Aggression in Relation to Emotional Development', in D. Winnicott, *Through Paediatrics to Psychoanalysis* (London: Hogarth Press, 1958).

WINNICOTT, D. (1963) 'Communicating and Not Communicating Leading to a Study of Certain Opposites', in D. Winnicott, *The Maturational Process and the Facilitating Environment* (London: Hogarth Press, 1965).

WOLFENSTEIN, E. (1989) *The Victims of Democracy* (London: Free Association Books).

YOUNG, R. (1989) 'Post-Modernism and the Subject', *Free Associations*, 16, pp. 81–96.

Index